CRISIS AND CONTINUITY

The Jewish Family in the 21st. Century

CRISIS AND CONTINUITY

The Jewish Family in the 21st. Century

edited by

Norman Linzer
Irving N. Levitz
David J. Schnall

KTAV Publishing House, Inc.
Hoboken, NJ

Library of Congress Cataloging-in-Publication Data

Crisis and continuity : the Jewish Family in the 21st century / edited by Norman
Linzer, Irving N. Levitz, David J. Schnall
    p.   cm.
    ISBN 0-88125-507-6 : $39.50. — ISBN 0-88125-508-4 : $19.95
    1. Jewish families—United States. 2. Interfaith marriage—United
States. I. Linzer, Norman. II. Levitz, Irving N. III. Schnall, David J.
HQ525.J4C75   1995
306.85'089924073—dc20   94–42914
                  CIP

Manufactured in the United States of America
KTAV Publishing House, 900 Jefferson Street, Hoboken NJ, 07030

We are grateful for the generous support of the
Atran Foundation.

CONTENTS

INTRODUCTION

The Jewish family continues to be the subject of public concern and intense scrutiny. Changes in Jewish family structure have generally mirrored those in the general population. There are more singles, later marriages, high rates of divorce and remarriage, family violence, including spousal and child abuse, and low fertility rates. Jewish alcoholics, homosexuals, and drug addicts have come "out of the closet." Intermarriages have increased to a rate of 52 percent in recent years. These demographic patterns have caused alarm on all levels of the organized Jewish community.

As the population ages, and more people live into their eighties and nineties, the four-generation family is placing particular stresses on adult children who are caught between the needs of their elderly parents and those of their children and grandchildren, their careers, and their retirement plans.

In addition to these trends, the 1990 National Jewish Population Study unearthed disturbing patterns that indicate serious declines in expressions of Jewish identity and affiliation. These include low rates of synagogue affiliation, ritual observance, and Jewish education for children, and 210,000 Jews who have converted to other religions.

To be sure, not all thinkers on the Jewish communal scene are alarmed by these developments. They point to signs of the "transformation" of Jewish life into new forms, and the success of outreach efforts underway to bring nonaffiliated and intermarried Jews into the Jewish community, resulting in increased membership in synagogues and other institutions.

Others are extremely perturbed and anticipate the decline of the Jewish population and the disappearance of a large percentage of Jews. These "survivalists" point to the trends cited and hold out little hope for a revival of Jewish life unless concerted efforts are made to strengthen Jewish family life and institutions. The term that characterizes the consciousness of the survivalists is "crisis." They assert that the Jewish family and community are in a crisis situation of major structural proportions, whose solutions remain elusive.

In order to elucidate and understand the nature of this crisis, a committee of the faculty of the Wurzweiler School of Social Work of Yeshiva University decided to sponsor a lecture series under the auspices of the Atran Foundation. Composed of Dr. Irving Levitz, Carl and Dorothy Bennett Professor of Pastoral Counseling, Dr. Norman Linzer, Samuel J. and Jean Sable Professor of Jewish Family Social Work, and Dr. David Schnall, Herbert H. Schiff Professor of Community Social Work, the committee selected the theme "Crises in the Contemporary Jewish Family."

Five lecturers presented original papers to students, faculty, and interested members of the Jewish community. Additional papers were written expressly for this volume by the faculty committee.

Norman Linzer begins by discussing the societal trend of deinstitutionalization which contributes to the expansion of choice and personal freedom, and the value conflicts of self vs. other, and rights vs. obligations that may explain rising divorce rates and low fertility rates.

Ruth Pinkenson Feldman presents an overview of the stress points affecting the modern Jewish family. As she makes clear, stresses exist in many different areas, including the family's economic stability and its struggle to maintain fiscal viability, marriage patterns and singlehood, the struggles of single parents to maintain an intact family, and the sandwich generation—the pressures on adult children who care for their own families and their elderly parents.

Rivka Ausubel Danzig focuses on the battered Jewish family. Thoroughly discussing its social and clinical implications, she uses case presentations as a medium for analyzing the forces battering the family that result in domestic violence, intermarriage, shattered unions and families, and intergenerational strife.

Francine Klagsbrun compares the changing roles taken on by today's Jewish women with their traditional roles, and the impact on two-parent and one-parent Jewish families. She finds strength in the ways Jewish women express their domestic, religious, and economic roles, and draws implications for Jewish communal responses.

Irving Levitz presents a psychological analysis of the differences between Jewish identity and Jewish identification, and argues that those with Jewish identities tend to intermarry less than those with Jewish identifications.

Mark Sirkin discusses the clinical aspects of intermarriage through theory and case material. He offers psychological insights into the decision to intermarry and conflicts with parents, and on the ethical issues that emerge when a service of Yeshiva University offers assistance on intermarriage between Jews and Gentiles.

Michael Salamon presents a demographic profile of the Jewish elderly. It includes age range, religiosity, patterns of acculturation, family roles and relationships, and the utilization of Jewish communal services.

David Schnall follows with a detailed discussion of issues related to caring for incapacitated parents. After tracing such classic Jewish sources as the Talmud, Maimonides' code, and other medieval authors regarding the scope of the responsibilities of adult children for ill parents, he draws implications for the role of adult children and the organized Jewish community today.

An epilogue integrates the themes in this volume and draws conclusions for the role of Jewish educational institutions and Jewish communal services.

Special gratitude is extended to Dr. Sheldon R. Gelman, Dorothy and David Schachne Dean of the Wurzweiler School of Social Work of Yeshiva University, for his wholehearted support for this venture.

Norman Linzer
Irving Levitz
David Schnall

April 1995

SELF AND OTHER:
THE JEWISH FAMILY IN CRISIS

Norman Linzer

Ever since the publication of the 1990 National Jewish Population Survey (Council of Jewish Federations 1991), both lay and professional leaders of the organized Jewish community have sounded the alarm about the erosion of Jewish life in the United States. Perhaps the most startling figure was the 52 percent intermarriage rate for those who have married since 1985, compared to a 6 percent rate for those who married before 1965.

The data also indicate the conversion of 210,000 Jews to other religions, a fertility rate of 0.87 children to those aged 25–34, reflecting a pattern of later marriage and postponement of childbearing. The number of singles and the rate of divorce have increased in recent years. Only 52 percent of born Jews say that being Jewish is very important in their lives.

The data regarding synagogue membership, Jewish education, and ritual performance also indicate a steady decline in the practice of Judaism and identification with Jewish life. Jews have become very Americanized and, in the process, have relinquished much that is distinctive in their religion and culture.

This presentation will examine some of the factors that have led to these social patterns, and will suggest ways of combating them. There are, however, no real solutions, for as long as Jews desire to be acculturated, the problems that accompany assimilationist tendencies will persist. But it behooves us to try to understand the state of affairs we are in through a conceptual and theoretical framework. This framework will then be applied to two vital indices of problems in family life: divorce and fertility. Implications will be drawn for the role of the organized Jewish community and, in particular, the rabbi.

1

PERSONAL FREEDOM AND THE RIGHT TO CHOOSE

The issue of personal freedom is central in discussions on the role of the family in modern society. The underlying concept of personal freedom suggests living with no constraints whatsoever. The childless family, as a corollary of this radical approach to freedom, is an extension of the deep-seated fear of relationships which limit the individual.

Family responsibilities tend to create restrictions on personal freedom by limiting individual choices and options. Having a child creates demands which shrink the area of personal freedom and independence. "Responsiveness, being limited by other human beings, the giving up of the understanding of freedom as unrestricted movement, are vital factors needed if modern man is to make sense of living in a moral universe" (Hartman, n.d.).

The notion of personal freedom is intricately tied with the process of the deinstitutionalization of modern society. This phenomenon refers to the weakening of the coercive power and moral authority of the institutional order. It comes about as a result of what Max Weber has called the rationalization and secularization of modern society. In this type of society, religion is demystified, means are more closely calculated to ends, and the institutions and traditions that were formerly taken for granted as ordering social life are questioned. Popper has coined the term "second-order tradition" for the attitude of questioning tradition (Popper 1965). When people ask questions about traditions, they can reaffirm them, but there is always a chance that they will reject them as transmitted, and alter them to suit their needs.

Questioning traditions and the moral authority of institutions is what occurs under conditions of deinstitutionalization. Institutions, by definition, order behavior and provide predictability in social relations. They provide a stable background in which human activity may proceed with a minimum of decision-making most of the time, and they free energy for such decisions as may be necessary on certain occasions (Berger and Luckmann

1967). In a heavily institutionalized, traditional society, institutions narrow choices for decision-making. The answer to the question "Why do you do it this way?" is, "Because my parents and grandparents did it this way."

In modern society, the institutions move from the background of consciousness, where they ordered behavior, to the foreground, where they are subject to question and challenge. Individuals believe that they have a right to flout the moral authority of institutions and to alter their patterns according to their own proclivities. The process of deinstitutionalization represents the supremacy of choice over authority and of personal freedom over responsibility.

The struggle between accepting the moral authority of institutions and challenging it under conditions of deinstitutionalization can be seen in the contrast between the traditional Jewish perspective on the family and the modern perspective.

In traditional societies, religion legitimated social institutions by bestowing an ontological status upon them, that is, by locating them within a sacred and cosmic frame of reference. Everything that is "here below" has its analogue "up above." For example, Judaism considers the human sexual act that results in the conception of a human being as a reflection of divine creativity. The court of justice is a *bet din shel matta* ("lower court"), analogous to the *bet din shel ma-ala* ("divine court"). The human family is a reflection of *pamalya shel ma-ala*, the divine family. The home is a *mikdash me'at*, a miniature sanctuary (Linzer 1974). Thus, by participating in the institutional order, people participate in the divine cosmos (Berger 1968).

In the traditional Jewish family, the recipe knowledge inherent in roles was transmitted generationally. Lines of authority and rewards and punishments were communicated to children by their parents, and were reinforced by the religious institution—Jewish law. With clarity of roles went consistency of behavior, leaving little room for decision-making. Family life, enveloped within the religious community, provided a bulwark of security which enabled the members to face the world.

The contemporary American family is immersed in a societal process of deinstitutionalization. It is quite alone. It does not have the firmness of support from other institutions or from a cohesive community. It has changed from traditional to companionship to existential (Polsky and Duberman). In the existential family, each individual gratifies his/her own need for self-development. Equality is the norm. Roles are created through the interaction of all the members and can be changed by agreement. The changing and reinterpretation of roles is common in a deinstitutionalized society where choices abound and decision-making becomes more complex.

As traditional family roles change, and family members decide how they want to interact with each other and the responsibilities they want to assume, they are thrown back on their own strengths and values. Since there are few objective guidelines for role changes in family life, parents invariably find themselves innovating to create behavioral norms and expectations for themselves and their children. They find it more difficult to make decisions, which can lead to inconsistency and confusion.

Families living under deinstitutionalized conditions where variations of family roles and expectations are numerous may find themselves torn apart by centrifugal forces beyond their control. These forces make it increasingly difficult for the family to fulfill its functions and to maintain stability, particularly when strong institutional and community supports are lacking (Linzer 1978).

IDEOLOGICAL CONFLICT

In addition to the decline of institutional authority as a major factor contributing to the attenuation of strong family ties, the Jewish family is confronted by a formidable conflict between Judaic values and secular values. The Jewish family can learn to deal with the decline of institutional authority by reinforcing parental authority with that of the halakhah (Jewish law). This presupposes the family's commitment to the traditional way of life through the study of Torah and the observance of mitzvot— acts that will support parental guidance of children when introduced with kindness and sensitivity. Families not committed to a traditional way of life can maintain authority through other means, which can be as effective.

Though parental authority may be intact, there is another area of potential disturbance that may wreak havoc on the fragile unity of the family. As most families are exposed to the majority culture, both parents and children imbibe many of its values in the course of daily living. Some of these values enrich the personality and expand horizons. Others provoke insidious behavior patterns that may lead to the dissolution of a close-knit family and an aversion to community.

SELF VS. OTHER

There is an ideological conflict between modern Western values and Judaic values that is located in the self vs. the other and rights vs. responsibilities. In the conflict of fulfilling the self vs. commitment to the other, there appears to be an ethos in Western culture that the needs of the self should take primacy. This is reflected in the preference for individual autonomy over physician paternalism in bioethical dilemmas, the value of self-determination and the goal of self-realization in the therapeutic enterprise, and in popular culture with magazines such as *SELF* that promote self-development for women.

The cultural emphasis on self seems also to have affected a change in the nature of Jewish identity. In the past, the common denominator of Jewish identity was a community of belief based on a system of shared values. Over the last century, however, the focus has shifted in the direction of a community of shared individual feelings.

The community of belief constituted a total system that controlled the individual's environment with a detailed pattern of prescribed actions and fixed roles. Group membership was thus clearly defined.

In contrast, the contemporary community of shared individual feelings is a voluntary and partial community of personal choice, with unclear boundaries and undefined membership. It is characterized by emotions and attachments, which, while often deep, are not always clearly articulated.

(Medding et al. 1992, p. 16)

The authors proceed to apply the concept of shared feelings to Jewish identity configurations in mixed marriages. Mixed-married couples see Jewish identity as a personal issue, and are convinced that participation in a mixed family—providing an experience of diversity and pluralism—may be deemed personally enriching. Neither partner's personal identity has to impinge on the other (p. 17).

Bulka (1982) has suggested that the ethic of self-realization is a major factor in divorce and low fertility rates among American families. The value placed on privacy in this society exacerbates the emphasis on self-absorption. Hendin (1976), too has observed that "the family becomes the center of concern for the ever-retreating prize of self-fulfillment." When this occurs, family members seem to move away from the center and do not attend sufficiently to each other's needs. They are much less willing to invest time and energy in promoting family life. The value placed on children has dropped, and it is not even clear that most adults feel personally fulfilled (Popenoe 1992).

What is needed to remedy this problematic situation is to emphasize the needs of the other, what Bulka calls "self-transcendence" and what Popenoe calls "self-sacrifice." In Judaism, these values are found in marriage and coalesce into the value of community. In the marital relationship, the husband is urged to honor his wife more than himself, and the wife is urged to honor her husband greatly (Maimonides, *Mishneh Torah*, Laws of

Women 15:19–20). For the husband, the wife's needs come first; for the wife, the husband's needs come first. They each come first for each other. When Jews give of themselves to others, they not only build and strengthen a marriage and a family, but they thereby build community. They are not isolated individuals whose world revolves around themselves. Their fortunes are intertwined with those of their people. In the words of Elie Wiesel (1977):

> What would the Jew be without his community? A withered branch. . . . By linking his own memory to that of his people, a Jew lives not outside time, detached from reality, but more deeply and at a level where all threads are woven together. He thus finds himself at home in every century.

There is a symbiotic relationship between the family and the community. Each needs the other in order to survive as a viable entity. The community is the family writ large, and it steps in when the family becomes dysfunctional. If the family is not successful in instilling values of the "other" into its members, there are important institutions in the Jewish community that can assist it in doing so. The synagogue, as the major religious institution, is the place where, in theory and in practice, the value of community is acted out. Other Jewish communal institutions, such as the Jewish community center (JCC), are more inclusive in their embrace of all Jews, regardless of denominational persuasion or belief. Many Jews see the JCC as the vehicle for promoting their Jewish identification and their belonging to the Jewish community. As a highly organized community, we possess the institutions and the knowledge and skill to assist individuals to foster identification with larger social units in order to transcend their preoccupation with themselves. Yet, we seem to be losing the battle for strengthening the ethic of self-sacrifice in family and community life.

RIGHTS VS. RESPONSIBILITIES

The emphasis on rights, in lieu of responsibilities, is similarly pervasive in this society, and is directly related to the conflict between self and other. The notion of rights abounds on all levels of social life. By "rights" we understand "that which a person has a just claim to; power, privilege, etc. that belongs to a person by law, nature or tradition" (*Webster's New World Dictionary*, 1957). These days everyone seems to have rights that demand gratification from others. Children have rights, patients have rights, homosexuals have rights, criminals have rights, students have rights—they all seem to have rights, and no one speaks of their responsibilities.

The ethic of rights presupposes a concentration on the self and the satisfaction of individual wants. The focus is on the individual's claims on others, entitlements owed by others to oneself. The "I" comes first. This ethos derives from the democratic principle of inalienable rights to life, liberty, and the pursuit of happiness which is symbolized in the Bill of Rights. Rights are endemic to American culture.

When diverse groups exercise their rights and their claims become strident, conflict may ensue. The ethic of responsibility is negated. With the negation of responsibility goes the diminution of caring. Communal and political responses focus on defusing the conflict by clarifying the rights of each group and stressing their overarching responsibilities to the community.

In the Jewish community, the ethos of rights can be destructive to planning, building, and strengthening Jewish life because it focuses on what the community owes individuals and groups, and not the reverse. To counteract it, community leaders—both lay and professional—will need to translate Jewish traditional values and behaviors into modern language and behavior. We teach responsibility when we expect children to respect their parents and elders, when we encourage people to give tzedakah, when we build institutions to meet vital communal needs. Here, too, we possess the knowledge, values, and skill to translate Jewish tradition in ways that speak to moderns and inspire them to put caring for others ahead of their personal claims on the community's largesse. This is not easily done, but neither can we desist from making the effort.

IMPLICATIONS FOR THE AMERICAN JEWISH FAMILY

Waxman (1983) has observed that, though certain unique family patterns persist, the American Jewish family has changed considerably from the traditional Jewish patterns and is increasingly manifesting the same patterns as the general American middle-class family. It is structurally incapable of carrying out enculturation on its own. In this connection, Feldman (1989) has noted a growing reversal in the relationship between families and the Jewish community. "Whereas in the past Jewish values and learning acquired in the family sustained the Jewish community, today Jewish communal institutions are being asked to preserve the family and to educate its members" (p. 1).

We noted earlier that social patterns that exist in the general community seem to be paralleled in the Jewish community. These include the rising rate of divorce and the low rate of fertility. The remainder of this presentation will analyze the incidence of divorce and fertility and the factors that contribute to their rise or fall.

DIVORCE

Although the divorce rate among couples who have been married a long time is greater than it used to be, it is the younger generation that sets the pace. The younger the couple, the more likely they are to divorce. Couples marrying today have less than a 50 percent chance of sustaining their marriage until the death of one of the partners. While these figures reflect the general population, there is consensus that the divorce rate among Jews is higher today than in the past (Waxman 1983).

There is a notable distinction, however, between the Orthodox and the non-Orthodox. Cohen (1989) has posited that those who are more religiously involved display more traditional family characteristics. Among Jews, traditionalism has been linked to higher fertility, lower intermarriage, and lower divorce rates. He asks what it is about the Orthodox that leads to such ostensibly positive family patterns. "Can, and should, Orthodox familism be emulated by, or 'exported' to non-Orthodox Jews? How do the Orthodox succeed in promoting marriage, in-marriage, stable marriage, and higher birth rates?" (p. 5).

The answer is obvious, and is contained in his opening statement. People who are more religiously involved tend to focus less on the satisfaction of their personal needs and on their own ego gratification, and to be more involved with the needs of others, be they family or community. The religious mentality requires the assumption of responsibility to perform mitzvot (duties), rather than claiming the satisfaction of rights.

It is, therefore, a relatively easy challenge to transfer this mentality to the need to marry early, to work successfully at preserving the marriage, to have many children, and to raise them in a home environment where their Jewish identity is strong.

EXPLANATIONS FOR DIVORCE

One way to make sense of the divorce trend, besides the idiosyncratic factors that affect individual couples in special ways, is to consider the broad social changes over the last generation.

- Women have entered the work force in great numbers. Their economic independence combined with their psychological independence make them far less likely to put up with a bad marriage than their mothers were.
- Men and women of the "me generation" are accustomed to having their needs met by the other person. When problems develop in the marriage, many of them abandon the relationship instead of

trying to keep it together.
- The romantic side of marriage exacerbated by the media has created unrealistic expectations in the young couple, who are unpre-
pared to face the harsh realities of day-to-day real-life
relationships.
- The disappearance of the social stigma of divorce has fostered the
attitude that it is a perfectly acceptable solution to a problematic
marriage, and does not reflect the personal failure of any of the
parties (*William Petschek National Jewish Family Center Newsletter*
1986).

These social trends will predictably continue. There is, though, a
glimmer of hope in the recent leveling off of divorce rates that
may bode well for the preservation of marriage. Greater efforts
are being expended by couples in conflict to try to resolve their
differences by seeking help from professionals. The struggle to
save a marriage represents the partners' attempt to transcend
themselves in the marital bond.

If values are used as a source of analysis, the divorce rate can be
explained through the emphasis on self-realization (Bulka 1982)
and the refusal or inability to view the marriage as encompassing
the individuals who comprise it. The exercise of rights may be
preferred over the proffer of responsibility. It is only when the
partners feel a sense of responsibility to work at their relationship
that the marriage can become a sacred canopy that envelops and
sustains them.

From a psychodynamic perspective, divorce can be attributed
to different psychological and psychosocial factors. Divorced
people usually blame the breakdown of their marriages on financial quarrels, physical and mental abuse, lifestyle conflicts, communication breakdown, and drifting apart. Divorce also tends to
correlate with depression, alcoholism, mental illness, and suicide—with a variety of emotional problems that may or may not
have preceded the marriage.

Another factor, which may be particularly pertinent to the Jewish family, is the couple's inability to separate from their respec-

tive parents. Separation from parents is a prerequisite for marriage (Gen. 2:24). This refers not only to physical distance but psychological independence. It does not entail severing ties, but requires creating enough distance for the couple to form new identities as husband and wife through their communication (Berger and Kellner 1970).

The lack of boundaries between the couple and their respective parents may help to explain the existence of marital conflict that could lead to divorce. Hertz and Rosen state: "After marriage, the connections and obligations to the extended family continue to be of great importance. Therefore, young Jewish couples typically spend a great deal of time defining the boundaries, connections, and obligations between themselves and their families" (1982, p. 366). When these ties are strong and parental ideologies and traditions are carried over to the marriage, conflict may ensue when the couple does not translate them to suit their relationship. They may find it difficult to change parental beliefs and practices because giving them up would appear to be a betrayal of their family of origin (Linzer 1986).

The betrayal may be particularly directed to the mother. In the traditional Jewish family, though not unique to it, the mother was the dominant figure. Being a mother meant the expenditure of greater emotional energy in care, concern, and worry for her children than being a wife to her husband. The new couple may feel guilty if they deviate from the behavioral norms of their families of origin. In addition, if mothers become too deeply involved in the lives of the newlyweds, the potential for conflict is rife.

Since there is a potential for divorce whenever marital conflict exists, we have merely highlighted one potential harbinger of conflict—the lack of clear boundaries between the new couple and their families of origin. The need for boundaries is manifested not only in the marital relationship, but also on a more macro level—in the relationship between an ethnic group and the larger society.

ETHNIC BOUNDARIES

It is a commonplace that minority groups are concerned with group size so that they can survive in the larger society as a distinct group. Preventing assimilation and maintaining replacement fertility patterns are among the ways they can achieve this objective. Jews have expended significant energy and resources to achieve both goals. The prevention of assimilation is the task of the socializing institutions in the community. Socialization represents the effort to maintain the group's internal boundaries.

It has been said that ethnic groups create double boundaries: a boundary from within maintained by the socialization process, and a boundary from without established by the process of intergroup relations (Stein and Hill 1977).

The internal boundary is designed to keep members from leaving the group; the external boundary is designed to keep people out of the group by excluding those who do not belong.

The internal boundary, maintained by socializing forces, is mainly the responsibility of the family, abetted by other institutions, such as religion and education. If the family is incapable of maintaining the boundary because it is subject to assimilationist forces, they will penetrate the porous boundaries of the group, weaken efforts at socialization and identity formation, and forestall the ability to perpetuate the group's existence. Assimilated families make it more difficult for the community to combat the forces that separate the family from its Jewish roots. When the family fails at socialization, many times the community will offer resources and programs, such as Jewish family education, to fill the gap, but success rates have been negligible.

FERTILITY PATTERNS

In addition to retarding the influence of assimilation, another means of maintaining group size is promoting fertility.

Over the years, with intermarriage rates steadily rising, marriages occurring later, and fertility rates falling, alarmist cries have been heard regarding the disappearance of American Jewry. As has often been noted, Jews have the most favorable attitudes toward the use of contraceptives, and use birth control to a greater extent and more efficiently than other groups (Waxman 1983).

It has been generally accepted that for a group to replace itself demographically, an average of 2.1 children is necessary. For American Jews, the issue is not that of zero population growth, but of negative population growth. The recent National Jewish Population Survey (Council of Jewish Federations 1991) found that the "Core Jewish Population has had low fertility over most of the past 40 years. By the end of childbearing years at age 45, Jewish women in the Core Population exceeded population replacement levels (2.1 children) only among those who became mothers at the height of the baby boom and are now in the age cohort 55–64" (p. 15). The survey also indicated that Core Jewish women delay childbearing until their late twenties and seem to continue it into their thirties. On the basis of the trends, it has been predicted that "The smaller cohorts born in the United States during the 1960s and the 1970s, among Jews as among total whites, will tend to reduce births in coming decades" (Schmeltz and Dellapergola 1988, p. 14).

FACTORS IN FERTILITY RATES

Three factors have been cited that have influenced the rates of fertility: educational attainment, employment of women, and minority status. "Among all white women aged 18–34 in 1985, fertility expectations declined with rising educational attainment—down to 1.77 for those with five or more years of college, 18 percent of whom expected to remain childless. Expectations were also lower for women in the labor force than for those not in it" (Schmeltz and Dellapergola 1988, p. 11). Waxman agrees that the increase of American Jewish women in the labor force accounts, to a large extent, for the declining birthrate of American Jews. In a couple's decision to have more than one child, a major consideration is the ability to negotiate the demands of work and the demands of childrearing (1983, p. 171).

Waxman disagrees with Goldscheider, who suggests that the minority status of Jews has been the cause of their low fertility, and, by inference, that if they become more acculturated and more economically secure, the birthrate will increase. He points out that American Jewry has been successful economically, has become acculturated and integrated into American society, and yet the birthrate has continued to decline. In fact, the birthrate is higher among the Orthodox, who are less acculturated and more visible as a minority, than the other groups.

In light of these factors—women's higher educational attainment and their increasing entry into the work force—"it is difficult to envision any significant changes in the fertility patterns of American Jews in the foreseeable future" (Waxman 1983, p. 173).

IDEOLOGICAL FACTORS

In addition to the sociological factors cited above, there may be ideological factors that could explain the low birthrate of American Jews. We have been discussing the prevalence of an ethos of personal freedom and self-realization under conditions of deinstitutionalization in American society. Its effect on everyday life has been the proliferation of choices that challenge the moral authority of established institutions, and throw the individual back upon him/herself to decide how to live and how to explain those decisions. This process may be personally freeing for some, because more options are available and they thrive on diversity. It may be anxiety-producing for others, for they may be unable to make the plethora of decisions required for everyday life.

In this society, the emphasis on self and rights, as opposed to other and obligations, throws individuals back upon themselves to decide whether and how many children to have. In the Jewish community, it is up to the couple, and the considerations are many, but one of them is not usually whether to subject themselves to the authority of Jewish law and to preserve the continuity of the Jewish people—the "other."

The Orthodox tend to have more children because as a mitzvah it is obligatory, and because they are concerned with the perpetuation of the group. The non-Orthodox tend to stress personal autonomy and historical change in matters of Jewish law. This mentality implies the right to choose in adhering to the tradition. Consequently, a wife's education and employment can be major factors in choosing whether and how many children to have, because children tend to interfere with, and limit, the personal freedom of marital partners.

IMPLICATIONS FOR THE ORGANIZED JEWISH COMMUNITY

We have selected for study two important indices that affect the strength and vitality of the Jewish family and, by extension, the Jewish community. Divorce and fertility patterns reflect varying degrees of commitment to marriage, to the needs of the other, and to obligations and sacrifices that transcend the self. These two demographic factors are only part of a larger schema of trends that give cause for worry to social scientists and communal leaders concerning the future direction of Jewish communal life.

Periodically, the organized Jewish community decries the depressing statistics that emanate from community and national studies that point to the erosion of Jewish life. Of late, attention has been riveted on intermarriage rates, which have seriously alarmed lay and professional leaders. The data inspired the leadership of the Council of Jewish Federations to devote a full day at their General Assembly in November 1992 to studying Jewish texts and ways of strengthening Jewish identity. A Commission on Jewish Identity was formed.

In recent years, there has been a vocal debate between two groups of Jewish social scientists—the transformationalists and the traditionalists—over the interpretation of the trends in Jewish life. The transformationalists, represented by Steven Cohen (1987) among others, maintain that the widespread identification, affiliation, and differentiation that exist in the Jewish community reflect the transformation of Jewish life into new forms that differ from those of the past. They are optimistic about the future.

The traditionalists, represented by Charles Liebman (1987), among others, offer a "grim outlook" on the future of American Jewish life. They point to the high intermarriage rates, the lack of serious commitment to Jewish education, the paucity of affiliation with synagogues and other institutions, and the decline in the practice of ritual as seriously eroding the quality and vitality of Jewish life. They are pessimistic about the future.

The organized Jewish community, as represented by its social and communal service agencies, does not seem to be as optimistic as the transformationalists would have it be. Agencies acknowledge that they are waging an uphill battle against the forces of assimilation, and losing. This is partly due to the fact that the leaders themselves are assimilated, and to the reality that American Jews prefer to live their lives as full-fledged members of this society. To maintain Jewish life and preserve the traditional values that served to perpetuate the group until the present requires the erection of boundaries high enough to foster a distinctive Jewish culture and identity. Modern Jews are not yet ready to erect boundaries that will, in effect, distinguish them and their culture and values from those of other Americans.

The efforts that have been made have been impressive. The federations' commitment to support Jewish education has been growing in recent years. The growth of all-day schools among the Conservative and Reform, as well as the Orthodox; the concerted emphasis on informal and formal Jewish education in the JCCs; the extensive efforts of Jewish outreach organizations; the expansion of Jewish courses on college campuses—all bode well for a possible renewal of Jewish commitment in the younger generation.

IMPLICATIONS FOR THE RABBI

The rabbi is not only a teacher, but also someone to whom the community turns when in need. Traditionally, the rabbi visited the sick, comforted mourners, and performed the rituals attending to the rites of passage through the life span.

In the nonritualistic realm, rabbis are not as prepared as they should be. When families are in trouble today, the rabbi can utilize neither rituals nor lectures to "fix" the problem. Many families need professional counseling, which most rabbis are not equipped to offer. Rabbis should not be doing counseling except on a short-term basis, and for the express purpose of making a referral.

Making a referral presupposes that the rabbi can discern the trouble spots in the family, and not deny that the family is in trouble. Signs of trouble abound in Jewish families today. The Orthodox family displays problematic behavior similar to other families, only less pronounced and public. The Jewish community has been wont to cover this up because it believes it should not be happening. The stereotypes are many: Jewish men do not beat their wives and children; Jewish men do not sexually abuse their children; Jewish men and women are not homosexuals or alcoholics, nor do they commit adultery; Jewish women do not neglect or beat their children, and so on. The longer the rabbi refuses to acknowledge that pathology exists in the community, the harder it will be to serve the needs of troubled families. Denial only serves to delay treatment.

In order to make a referral, the rabbi needs to get to know the executive director and the key staff of the local Jewish family service agency, as well as professional social workers and psychologists in private practice. One needs to know to whom one is referring the particular individual, couple, or family—the professional's credentials, experience, specialization, and commitment to Jewish life.

The rabbi's greatest strength, however, is in the knowledge of Judaism and as a representative of the Torah tradition. The rabbi lives and breathes Jewish values, and tries to convey them through model behavior. Dedication to the service of the community and the ability to teach the concept of mitzvah as obligation should ideally set an example for congregants. Preoccupation with self has no place in the Jewish community where the needs of helping others, including one's spouse and children, Jewish day schools, and people who have lost their jobs and who are ill, should be paramount. The rabbi must be in the forefront of the community to combat the American values of self and rights over other and obligations.

CONCLUSION

To be a Jew in America at the end of the twentieth century is to fight an uphill battle to preserve the values that have preserved the Jewish community since the beginning of time. One of these values is concern for the other. This is expressed in the assumption of responsibility for the needs of the community, the establishment of mutual aid societies, performing the central mitzvot of tzedakah and hessed that have contributed to making the Jewish community a caring community.

In families, parents have always put the needs of their children first. The value placed on their work and study was secondary to the value of family, of raising children to be *mentschen* (proper adults).

These traditional values seem to have been overwhelmed by the dominance of values that propagate the self. The self has become primary. This has complicated efforts by the organized Jewish community to stem the tide of divorce, low fertility, intermarriage, nonaffiliation—signs of the erosion of Jewish life. While some social scientists may interpret these trends as part of the process of the transformation of Jewish life, others view them as grim reminders that we are in danger of losing our direction and purpose.

There are no easy solutions. For some, aliyah is the answer. For others, the effort to combat assimilation on the level of values must continue. It begins with one's own family and then it spreads to one's community. As concerned Jews, our reach must exceed our grasp.

REFERENCES

Berger, P. L. 1968. *The Sacred Canopy*. New York: Doubleday.

————, and Kellner, H. 1970. Marriage and the construction of reality. In *Recent Sociology No. 2*, ed. H. P. Dreitzel. New York: Macmillan.

————, and Luckmann, T. 1967. *The Social Construction of Reality*. New York: Doubleday Anchor.

Bulka, R. 1982. The Jewish family: Realities and prospects." *Jewish Life*.

Cohen, S. M. 1987. Reason for optimism. In *The Quality of American Jewish Life: Two Views*. New York: American Jewish Committee.

————. 1989. *Alternative Families in the Jewish Community*. New York: American Jewish Committee.

Feldman, R. P. 1989. *Child Care in Jewish Family Policy*. New York: American Jewish Committee.

Hartman, D. n.d. The challenge of family. Jerusalem: *Newsletter of the Shalom Hartman Institute for Advanced Judaic Studies*.

Hertz, F. M., and Rosen, E. J. 1982. Jewish families. In *Ethnicity and Family Therapy*, ed. M. McGoldrick, J. K. Pearce, and J. Giordano. New York: Guilford.

Liebman, C. S. 1987. A grim outlook. In *The Quality of American Jewish Life: Two Views*. New York: American Jewish Committee.

Linzer, N. 1976. *The Nature of Man in Judaism and Social Work*. New York: Federation of Jewish Philanthropies.

———. 1986. Philosophical reflections on Jewish family life. *Journal of Jewish Communal Service* 64, no. 2: 318–327.

Medding, P. Y., Tobin, G. A., Fishman, S. B., and Rimor, M. 1992. *Jewish Identity in Conversionary and Mixed Marriages*. New York: American Jewish Committee.

Council of Jewish Federations. *National Jewish Population Study*. 1991. New York: Council of Jewish Federations.

Polsky, H. W., and Duberman, L. n.d. The changing American family: From traditional to companionship to existential (typewritten).

Popenoe, D. 1992. The controversial truth: Two-parent families are better. *New York Times*. Dec. 12.

Popper, K. 1962. Toward a rational theory of tradition. In *Conjectures and Refutations*. New York: Basic Books.

Schmeltz, U. O., and Dellapergola, S. 1988. *Basic Trends in American Jewish Demography*. New York: American Jewish Committee.

Stein, H., and Hill, R. 1977. *The Ethnic Imperative*. Philadelphia: University of Pennsylvania Press.

Waxman, C. I. 1983. *America's Jews in Transition*. Philadelphia: Temple University Press.

Wiesel, Eli. 1977. United Jewish Appeal. *New York Times*. May 15.

Willaim Petschek National Jewish Family Center Newsletter. 1986.

STRESS POINTS IN THE CONTEMPORARY JEWISH FAMILY

Ruth Pinkenson Feldman

There have always been stress points in Jewish family life.[1] From the lessons learned from the internal dynamics of the families in Genesis through the dislocations and separation of families and the subsequent turmoil of the immigrant generation of this century,[2] Jewish families have endured through spiritual, social, and physical challenge. It has been said that in contemporary American society, the predominant struggle is to balance work and family. Perhaps we can more fruitfully view the particular stress points for the contemporary Jewish family by reformulating that struggle to issues, not only of balance, but of purpose. How and why do families build relationships, negotiate life's transitions, engage in meaningful work, and support and participate in community endeavors? Stress points for Jewish families are heightened, but may also be ameliorated, when family members attempt to establish a balancing between work and family, and take time to consider the ultimate purpose, from a Jewish perspective, of both work and family in contemporary American society.[3]

In this chapter we will look at three major life-cycle stages: marriage and singlehood, parenting, and the "sandwich generation," along with the pervasive issue of economics, briefly highlighting examples from each stage which demonstrate the tensions that contemporary Jewish families may experience, paying particular attention to the impact of these changes on families committed to Jewish tradition.[4]

Demographic statistics emerging from the CJF National Jewish Population Survey of 1990 reveal that the current American Jewish population reflects many of the structural patterns of contemporary society.[5] At any point in time, most Jews, like most

23

other Americans, do not live in households made up of a mother, father, and children. Such factors as increased longevity, delayed marriage, and higher divorce rates and thus the increase of single-parent families have contributed to a situation where demographers now report that most Jews, like most Americans, live either alone or in patterns other than the traditionally structured nuclear family unit. "Most significant, the proportion of traditional Jewish families is small. Of all households, 16 percent are composed of a married couple, both of whom are Core Jews and only 14 percent contain a Core Jewish married couple with children."[6] This particular statistic, of the small percentage of Jewish households traditional in structure, relates to household composition, not traditional Jewish practice. It is frequently overshadowed by the statement which follows it: "By contrast, 13 percent contain an interfaith couple with children. Such mixed households seem to be the fastest growing household type."[7] Thus, not only is the structural composition undergoing significant change, so too is the definition of "Jewish" and what is meant by "Jewish household."[8]

Access to educational opportunity and widening career choices have also contributed to a changing family structure, such that extended families often stretch across the continental United States. Even individuals within the nuclear family may live apart, with spouses commuting between different states, and/or children living alternately between two houses in shared-custody arrangements. It is also normative in America (and particularly in the Jewish community) for families to send college-age "children" away from home to schools all over the country and abroad. In many religiously traditional Jewish families this practice extends to younger adolescence, when many boys, and an increasing number of girls, are sent to out-of-town yeshivas and high schools, spreading the nuclear family across the United States or even to Israel.

Along with these changes in the "structure" of the basic family unit, the internal functioning has changed as well. Roles such as wage-earner, homemaker, student, professional, nurturer, primary caretaker, and custodial parent are now shared in new ways between spouses, often alternated over the course of a marriage, and are completely taken on by a growing number of single parents. In the traditional Jewish community, where the structure of the family unit is clearly defined and parental and religious gender roles and responsibilities delineated, deviations from the norm may be even more stressful for the individuals involved, their families, and the community itself. On the other hand, religious tradition and the sense of community surrounding it can provide a stabilizing influence in this transitional generation.

As the fabric of the Jewish community undergoes significant changes, it is often in the interrelationship between families and the community that stress points may be experienced as normative crises. Individuals feel these normative dilemmas when measuring themselves against others in a similar position or situation.[10] The tighter the community, the more stringently the norms are followed and the more stressful deviation becomes. In addition to these normative conflicts, issues of identity abound. Internalized role models of one's parents' lives may conflict with the options presented to, or decisions made by, young adults in the formative stages of their lives as individuals, as well as when they embark on the first stages of family formation.

In contemporary American society, where norms change rapidly, and in the Jewish community, where norms have changed radically within a generation, individuals may experience tremendous stress as the lives they embark on as adults are significantly different from those their parents modeled. In addition, an individual's understanding (or lack of understanding) of Jewish values and Jewish living may magnify the perceived stress, spur creative solutions to conflicts between Jewish tradition and modern life, or help to reconcile one's particular life circumstances within the traditional and changing norms of the community.

The Jewish family of past generations was charged with the responsibility of Jewishly educating the children (sons), enabling them to attain the skills of a trade or profession, and finding appropriate marriage partners for them.[11] The enculturation process, and with it the development of Jewish identity, happened generation to generation, parent to child, often within the extended family. Teaching and "learning" meant Jewish learning, learning Torah; and learning to live meant learning to live within the Jewish community. Jewish tradition taught the value of learning, honoring one's parents, respecting the elderly, caring for the widow, the orphan, and the poor. Those who could not teach their children were required to engage someone else to fulfill this important obligation.[12] When Jews moved from one place to the next, they immediately and routinely established the communal institutions they needed in order to live their lives as Jews. As such, they designated places to be used as a house of worship, a house of study, a mikva, and a cemetery. These communal institutions were created by Jews who knew what it was they needed to live together as Jews, as families, and as a community. Hevrot were also maintained, informal societies to provide for travelers' aid, clothing the needy, caring for the sick, dowering brides, and preparing the dead for the grave.

Today, in many communities, we are witnessing a reversal in this long-standing relationship where knowledgeable Jews created institutions to support their lives as Jews. In contemporary American society, communal secondary institutions are asked to "establish" the Jewish lives for many families.[13] Secondary institutions, such as schools, synagogues, and community centers, are given the function of institutions of socialization, charged not only with the (Jewish) education of the children, but with the task of defining the Jewish family and its function. Jewish community centers are shifting their emphasis from social and recreational goals to those of enhancing the Jewish identity, learning, and affiliation of their members. Synagogues themselves are confronting outreach issues of including the unaffiliated and even the intermarried.

Two cautions should be noted. First, the potential for conflict between the generations and between denominations may be heightened when the values learned in the community's secondary institutions conflict with, or are not strongly supported by, the home environment and/or the rest of the community. Second, a Jewishness that is increasingly defined by, and a result of, membership and affiliation is also increasingly subject to external factors, such as one's ability to financially participate in the community's institutions. Such barriers are very powerful in a kehillah which is dependent upon voluntary membership.

In fact, in a recent study on the high cost of Jewish living, the authors found that for a family of five who enroll their children in Jewish day school or child care, belong to a synagogue and to a Jewish community center, the combined annual costs could range from $15,000 to $25,000.[14] Such sums would require an annual household income of close to or over $100,000 before taxes. From another study during the same time frame, commissioned by the Council of Jewish Federations, we learn that 90 percent of Jewish households had incomes below $80,000 and 70 percent had incomes below $70,000.[15] Clearly, the economics of Jewish living must be reckoned with by community leaders. It was beyond the scope of the above-mentioned studies to deal with the complex interactions of values which may determine how and when discretionary income fosters or inhibits religious identity and affiliation. On the one hand, a commitment to observe halacha can add to the overload of today's families (preparations for Shabbat and holidays, day school tuition, the increased cost of kosher foods, inflated real estate values near synagogues, etc.). On the other hand, traditional Judaism provides a strong community, rules of ritual and ethical behavior, structure for negotiating life's transitions, and the sacred time throughout the year and in every week for families to relax, "refuel," and reflect on the ultimate purpose of their lives.

MARRIAGE AND SINGLEHOOD

The covenantal bond of Jewish family life is the basis for having children, establishing a Jewish home, and sustaining the continuity of the Jewish community. Understanding this as a Jewish value may motivate those in a position either to marry early or to postpone marriage and family. The functional dimensions of marriage in contemporary society have changed rapidly since the women's movement, which began in the early seventies. Today, Jewish women are the most likely of all American women to attain high educational and professional achievements and feel many of the same pressures which their "brothers" experienced in earlier years to succeed in prestigious careers. Pressures mount to sustain both family and work responsibilities. Balancing family and career requires constant renegotiation by the partners in a marriage when each was raised in a home where men and women had specific roles. Men are expected not only to sustain the achievement level of their fathers, but also to share household responsibilities. Major shifts in role definitions will take more than a generation to accomplish, and changes continue to occur as individuals seek to correct what they perceive as the injustices of their lives. Understanding that one of the functions of the marriage is to create a Jewish home can serve to galvanize a family's collective capacity to work together to prepare for Shabbat so that the entire responsibility does not fall on the wife or mother. As children grow and develop, they too can participate in the family's efforts to create a Jewish home together. A marriage can model the view that the "covenantal relationship" between husband and wife is of a higher value than the self-actualization of either of the partners.

One example of a normative dilemma concerning the issue of marriage is that of the "expected" age of marriage for individuals within a community. Norms vary greatly between communities, and different expectations exist for men and women.

Judaism has always placed a high value on marriage and family. However, the very high value that the Jewish community gives to marriage may place enormous feelings of insecurity and guilt on those in the community who are single by chance or by choice. This is particularly true for women, since they may not be viewed as favorably as single men, who have an important public role in synagogue life and represent a much smaller percentage of the community than single Jewish women.[16] As longevity increases, the likelihood that more people will experience some period of their adult lives as singles is increased (as is the opportunity for marriage and remarriage).

PARENTING ISSUES

The high value placed upon parenting is evident in the first mitzvah set forth in the Bible, "Be fruitful and multiply."[17] The birth of children brings the potential for tremendous joy, but can also be a source of stress. The earliest stress is that of infertility. The population survey confirmed a high incidence of infertility in married Jewish couples. Pursuing medical alternatives along with proper halachic guidance and support can help a couple through this highly personal and emotional time. The increase in adoptions and the rise in the number of foreign-born adopted children being raised as Jews provides a challenge to the entire Jewish community to deal sensitively and inclusively with the changing faces of the Jewish community.

One issue facing many Jewish families is the cost factor of Jewish education, which has become a major burden for parents across all income ranges. The costs of formal and informal Jewish education are very high even in relation to national averages for incomes in the Jewish community. Some parents who would like to enroll their children in Jewish schools cannot do so for financial reasons. This is also a reflection of different philosophies of community funding and of the policies of the schools themselves. Some schools take the position that all Jewish children are entitled to a Jewish education, and provide extensive scholarships to all who seek admission. Other community-based day schools subscribe to a policy which equates day school education with private schooling, and essentially recruit and cater to a population that can afford private education, with a less extensive scholarship base. Ironically, an increasing number of Jewish educators and communal workers are in the income range where they do not qualify for financial aid but without it cannot afford day schools for their children.

Families with many children are under enormous pressures. On the lower income level, economic stress may lead to an inability to invite guests for Shabbat or holiday meals; others may have difficulty clothing large (and small) families with both weekday clothes and shoes and special outfits for Shabbat and the hagim. Even middle-income parents may find themselves resentful and frustrated over their long work hours and their inability to buy furniture or purchase a home if they continue to pay full tuition, much less take family trips to Israel or send children to summer camps. Economic stress may be relative, but for each person, and each family's situation, the concerns are legitimate. At what point does a relatively high-income professional family, paying for, say, five children to attend day schools or yeshivot, feel they can legitimately ask for help? And, if they continue to pay an annual cost of $40,000 or $50,000 for tuition, how do they balance their own need to save for their family's financial future against what they know are other families' greater immediate needs?

Another issue faced by many parents is that strong feelings heretofore unexpressed in a relationship may be elicited when it comes to religious experiences and educational opportunities for children. For instance, for parents who did not grow up in a world where adolescents routinely left home to attend yeshivas, such a choice might appear contradictory to their own experience as well as to normative patterns of adolescent development in mainstream America. Ironically, such a practice would appear normative in the upper classes of white Protestant society here and in England.

The choices which parents make in terms of their children's education have major ramifications not only for the child's life, but for that of the family. We know that just enrolling young children in Jewish day care can affect the Jewish identity of the family.[18] How much more so might choices for high school education have far-reaching effects. The separate and at times conflicting value systems which parents subscribe to for sons and daughters may even divide siblings within the same family.

Decisions that parents make for their children's high school education can and will have an impact on future choices of higher education, mates, and religious and/or secular orientation as these adolescents enter adulthood. Parents' choices for their children's Jewish education are further complicated if their child or children have learning difficulties or other special needs. The Jewish community is just beginning to recognize and meet the growing need for specialized programs to provide Jewish education within a Jewish framework for all of its children.

Through the younger generations' participation in schooling, youth groups, or camps, children may make greater demands on their families to learn and grow Jewishly along with them. For example, as a result of the baal teshuvah movement among a minority of college-age students, and as a growing number of young adults turn toward traditional Judaism,[19] parents may be unfamiliar with Jewish practice and may be asked to accommodate to their children's yearnings for a more intensive experience of Judaism. Some parents may feel threatened if their child knows more (Jewishly) than they do. Leaders of Jewish educational and communal settings must be willing to explore the potential among parents to provide support systems, mechanisms to participate in the community, opportunities for intergenerational learning and parent education. Unfortunately, heightened tensions can develop between generations and between young or even adult siblings as a result of different directions in learning and practicing the very Judaism which might otherwise bind them together.

Other parenting issues are highlighted when single-parent families are analyzed. Single parents in the Jewish community share the same concerns and conflicts as all Jewish parents, with the increased potential for economic pressures beyond those already felt by two-parent families. Single parents must also balance their own needs as individuals against the responsibilities of being a parent. Single parents and their children need opportunities to be part of the general "extended family" of the Jewish community. At other times, specific social and/or financial supports may be necessary to help cover the cost of participating in communal institutions or of being in an emotionally supportive situation with other single-parent families, or with other single parents.

As a result of the higher incidence of divorce in families with children, the structure of the parent-child relationship is modified for many by the court system. Options for joint custody of children, custodial parents, visitation rights, and vacation and holiday schedules illustrate dilemmas many families regularly face. Negotiating a relationship outside the daily routine of family life, and frequently outside the child's physical home, can challenge any parent. Frequently the issue of religion is a point of contention between the separated or divorced parents. Preferences for Jewish schools and Jewish camping experiences, and paying their costs, need to be specified in the divorce proceedings, but too often are not. When parents remarry, the religious orientation of the new spouse (or family, in the case of the blended family) must be reconciled.

Intergenerational financial assistance is often a two-way street. While there are certainly many elderly people who are financially supported by the "sandwich generation," in an increasing number of families the grandparent generation is both emotionally and financially supporting the single and/or divorced child and his/her children.

SANDWICH GENERATION

The term "sandwich generation" refers to those adults who are concurrently caring for their children and their parents, grandparents and or other elderly relatives. The stress of the competing needs, be they economic or emotional, between supporting one's parents or one's children may create significant conflicts.

Just as Judaism teaches a parent's responsibility to educate the child, the tradition is even more direct with regard to the obligations children have to their parents. However, it is really as an adult (child) that many of the obligations of reverence and honor to the parent are actualized. As Gerald Blidstein makes clear in his extensive treatment of the subject, these obligations are categorical and not calendrical.[20]

Changes in the demographic patterns of American Jewry have resulted in a number of fundamental shifts in our ways of taking care of an elderly parent. First, the romantic notion that in previous generations three generations routinely lived together, taking care of the elders, is not necessarily accurate in regard to long-term care. In general, Jews today live much longer. Those who are impaired either physically or mentally also live much longer and often require long-term sustained care. Simply put, in earlier times people did not live as long, and if they got sick, they were more likely to die. As medical care and work conditions improved dramatically, people in general, and Jewish people in particular, live much longer. In fact, this is the first generation to really be taking care of two generations of the elderly, the "young old" and the "old old" (those over seventy-five). The baby boom generation, now in its forties, actually represents the largest percentage of the population and, with its pattern of delayed marriage and childbearing, now finds many of its cohorts in the position of taking care of young children and caring for an aging population of their own parents.

One severe crisis point for those in the sandwich generation is a result of the very successes many encountered over the past few decades. It is the physical distancing between the generations as a result of migration.[22] Many members of the sandwich generation pursued career advancements and educational opportunities which took them far from their parental homes. Even though studies show that adult Jewish children speak with their elder parents more frequently on the telephone and have more contact with them than non-Jews, when the time comes for decisions about long-term care, such communication is not adequate to deal with the issues at hand. These issues often involve an intricate parent-child role reversal which is emotionally wrenching and physically and emotionally draining. For the older population, many who could afford to, left their homes for retirement communities. As parents age, many adult children, with the best of intentions, bring their parents to the very suburbs where they have established homes, but in so doing they may separate the parents from their own friends, doctors, and communal supports.

It is unclear how broadly the very commandment to honor one's parents may be interpreted in terms of responsibility for the provision of day-to-day physical care of a parent by the child, or by another caregiver paid by the child.[23] However, in studies comparing Jews with non-Jews (White Protestant, Catholic, and Afro-Protestant), Jews were found to use formal services at a significantly higher rate than non-Jews. Various ethnic groups agree on the son's managing the financial resources of aging parents, but the role of the daughter differs between groups. The Irish, for instance, take great pride in a daughter's personally caring for the physical needs of her aging parent. However, both Jewish mothers and daughters agreed that they would prefer that such physical care not be taken on by a family member. This may be explained by the general preference shown by Jews toward reliance on professional services. Another study revealed that regardless of financial status, and regardless of level of impairment, Jews still used paid services for their elderly parents at a higher rate than other ethnic populations.[24]

In a review of the literature on the Jewish elderly, Allen Glicksman found that "being Jewish has a definite impact on the experience of aging. This is a result of the early socialization of these aging individuals to Jewish values and lifestyles. These influences affect individuals throughout the life span in such areas as marriage, occupation, residence, and even use of medical services. In old age, life decisions continue to be decisively influenced by early socialization."[25]

CONCLUSION

There is no question that the very "success" of life in America for Jews is a constant challenge to traditional life as a Jew. Jewish families, like all families, experience the challenges of living in a transitional generation. Families for whom Jewish identity, identification, and continuity are salient may experience additional stresses as the Jewishness of their lives intersects and sometimes clashes with the values of American society.

When a child is raised in a home where Jewish values and the values of the family are one and the same, s/he learns to value and love what the parent does, just as s/he learns to value and love the parent. While a traditional Jewish home life and family structure cannot guarantee emotional and financial stability, the extended family of the traditional Jewish community is there to support those who are dealing with some of the turmoil caused by the structural and functional changes in the contemporary family.

It is hoped by this writer that the search for "what to do" to ease the crises within the lives of so many Jewish families, and the growing number of questions from across the denominations of "what's the Jewish way to deal with . . . ?" will eventually lead to an enriched religious community where many will find the support necessary to work through the traumas of their own lives while ensuring the stability of the Jewish community.

REFERENCES

1. There is a rapidly increasing genre of literature published by members of the Orthodox rabbinate to deal with many of the dilemmas in this chapter, e.g., *Jewish Divorce Ethics* by Reuven Bulka and *On Becoming a Jew* by Maurice Lamm.

2. Irving Howe, *World of Our Fathers* (New York: Simon & Schuster, 1976).

3. Religious diversity in the contemporary Jewish community makes it almost impossible to describe a "typical" Jewish family. However, despite the fact that religious differences between the denominations may make the Jewish practices of some families completely unrecognizable to others in the Jewish community, all Jewish families experience the stages of the Jewish life-cycle, and it is to this commonality among all Jews that this chapter is directed.

4. I am extremely grateful to Professor Rela Geffen for her careful reading of this chapter and to the hours of conversation with her which helped me to crystallize many of the ideas presented here.

5. Barry A. Kosmin, *Highlights of the CJF 1990 National Jewish Population Survey* (New York: Council of Jewish Federations in association with the Mandell Berman Institute–North American Data Bank, Graduate School and University Center, City University of New York, 1991).

6. Ibid.

7. Ibid.

8. The complex issues concerning intermarriage are beyond the scope of this chapter. Suffice it to say that the stress within families confronting intermarriage extends to the entire extended family, and to the community. Decisions to convert to Judaism may increase concerns as various family members may differ along denominational lines. One result is that conversion is now a subject being dealt with by all the movements, albeit in different ways.

9. Rela Geffen Monson, *Jewish Women On the Way Up* (New York: Ameri-

can Jewish Committee, 1987).

10. Rappaport and Rappaport, *Dual-Career Families* (Harmondsworth: Penguin Books, 1971); idem, *Dual-Career Families Reexamined: New Integration of Work and Family* (New York: Harper & Row, 1976).

11. Babylonian Talmud, Kiddushin 29a.

12. Maimonides, Mishneh Torah, Hilchot Talmud Torah 1:3.

13. Rela G. Monson, "The User Friendly Synagogue," *Conservative Judaism*, 1985.

14. Rela Gellen Monson and Ruth Pinkenson Feldman, "The Cost of Living Jewishly in Philadelphia," *Journal of Jewish Communal Service* 68, no. 2 (Winter 1991–92).

15. Kosmin, *Highlights of the CJF 1990 National Jewish Population Survey.*

16. Options in the structure of marriage are sensitively described from individuals' personal perspectives in *Jewish Marital Status* by Carol Diament (Jason Aronson, 1989), a book commissioned by the education committee of Hadassah. Attempting to portray what is happening in the Jewish community at large, along with presenting traditional Jewish sources, the book delineates the broad scope of options found today in the American Jewish community. Included are: single, not quite married, married, single again (widowed, abandoned, divorced), remarried, intermarried, gay or lesbian, and childless. Some of these stages create stress points both for the families involved and for the community at large as individuals seek recognition, participation, and legitimacy within the communal structures.

17. Genesis 1:28.

18. Ruth Pinkenson, "Impact of Jewish Day Care on Parental Jewish Identity" (Ph.D. diss., Temple University, 1987).

19. M. Herbert Danzger, *Returning to Judaism: The Contemporary Revival of Orthodox Judaism* (New Haven: Yale University Press, 1989).

20. Gerald Blidstein, *Honor Thy Father and Mother: Filial Responsibility in Jewish Law and Ethics* (New York: Ktav, 1975).

21. Allen Glicksman, *The New Jewish Elderly: A Literature Review* (New York: American Jewish Committee, Institute for Human Relations, 1991).

22. Parents may have been thrilled to watch their children attain professional degrees and career advancements, not realizing this would eventually result in a situation where the beloved child now lives across the country. Similarly, the "successful" and grateful (adult) child might not have imagined the matriarch of his family living alone in an aging community. The reader is referred to Blidstein's extensive treatment of this topic.

23. Allen Glicksman, Tanya Koropeckyj-Cox, Margaret Perkinson, and Steven Albert, "The Impact of Cultural Diversity on Caregiving" (Paper pre-

sented at annual meeting of Association for Gerontology in Higher Education, Baltimore, February 1992).

24. Allen Glicksman, "American Jews and Caregiving for the Aged" (Paper presented at 21st annual meeting of Association for Jewish Studies, Boston, December 1989).

25. Glicksman, *New Jewish Elderly,* p. vii.

THE BATTERED JEWISH FAMILY: SOCIAL AND CLINICAL IMPLICATIONS

Rivka Ausubel Danzig

The family qua family is in crisis, and now the Jewish family is in crisis as well. Definitions, configurations, and locations of families are changing continually, and rapidly. Stress abounds as economic problems and social uncertainties strike even those who used to seem protected from these woes. In fact, it seems that the family is today under more stress than ever before, and that the sense of being battered is pervasive.

C. Henry Kempe defines a battered child as one "who does not cry when he is stuck with a needle, is either very sick with his basic illness, or he is very sick emotionally, because he has been trained at home not to cry when he is hurt."[1] Is the Jewish family today so stuck with hurt and struck by stressors that it cannot even cry or cry out?

In the previous chapter, Ruth Pinkenson Feldman focused on major stress points in marriage, such as childbearing and fertility issues, growing up and individuating as adults, restructuring the roles of men and women in the nuclear and extended family and in the marketplace, intermarriage and the potential ensuant ideological and religious clashes between couples and their extended families. The quest for survival is stressful in and of itself. It is compounded many-fold by the multiple attendant role requirements of employment, parenting, partnerships, and friendships. In addition, numerous stresses exist related to the status of singlehood, single parenting, and the sandwich generation wherein

---

Dedicated to the memories of Wurzweiler School of Social Work Professor Murray Raim and Adjunct Professor Miriam Mishkoff. May they rest in peace.

39

people are caught in the middle of taking care of children and parents.

These stress points can yield substantial angst and manifold crises for the Jewish family and its members. Add to these stress points a group of "battering forces," and what will emerge in this chapter is a composite picture of the battered Jewish family.

The notion of the battered Jewish family is based on the assumption that battering forces for the modern "besieged" family also apply to the Jewish family.[2] External forces include physical disease and mental illness, alcoholism and other kinds of addictions, gambling, and domestic violence, unemployment and economic hardship, and various forms of discrimination and harassment.

The battering forces specific to the Jewish family now in crisis are being termed "internal battering forces."[3] Unfortunately, it does not appear that Jewish families have been spared many of the above afflictions or external battering forces. Perhaps it is just a matter of degree or frequency as to how hard they are hit. In addition, Jewish families suffer from specific internal battering.

The focus of this chapter, then, is an examination of the nexus of external and internal battering forces for the Jewish family, in the framework of stressful life events, the study of life event webs, and the notion of ways people know what they know. Case material is brought to inform and illustrate these concepts to paint a beginning picture of the battered Jewish family.

STRESSFUL LIFE EVENTS

A critical or stressful life event is an asynchrony between change within an individual and change within the environment. This is experienced by the individual as a significant life event. The interaction between the individual and the situation may be perceived as special, stressful, or a critical life event.

Systems theory and eco-life-model theories suggest that stressful life events inevitably affect other interdependent lives, e.g., family members of spouses or children of these people.[4] "Life-event webs" capture the intricate linkage of individual lives.[5] This connotes the adaptation of entangled lives to respond to multiple forces, events, and changes.

It is useful to consider critical life events and their ripple effects in a developmental, longitudinal, or life span perspective. This implies that change is ongoing, and intersecting with many others over the course of life's different phases and passages. Hagestad views the family as a unique "life-span reflector," i.e., members of families observe others in life stages, and thus anticipate the joys and sorrows of phases to come. This he called "anticipatory socialization" of families as partners in "life-event webs."[6]

This may be exemplified by middle-aged children who find their parents' failing health painful because it sparks their own anticipation, anxiety, and dread about the future. It also contributes to what Wolin and Bennett have called the "family identity," its collective sense of self.[7]

For centuries, Jews lived in close proximity to one another, and relied upon each other. Children in Jewish families grew up with these "life-support webs," and always assumed that such a physical network would continue to exist. Regardless of the particular denomination of Judaism, the sights, smells, and tastes of childhood forged palpable memories that they always assumed would be theirs to transmit to their own children. Anticipatory socialization was in full bloom—they knew this with all their hearts! They knew they were the "People of the Book," and they knew that they were connected. Connected to an Other, be it to a divine Other, a Jewish historical context, and/or to significant human others.[8]

This kind of special knowing is akin to the definitions of knowing developed at the Stone Center for Women's Studies at Wellsley College.[9] What constitutes knowledge and, in particular, the concepts of subjective knowledge, procedural knowledge, and separate and connected knowing have been explored precisely in terms of the notions of interdependence and connectedness with others.[10]

Of late, the knowledge of connectedness has begun to erode for Jews. With the loosening of familiar boundaries and webs, some have become marginal people in marginal situations.[11] Their anticipatory socialization about ongoing Jewish values, observances, principles, and practices has changed. Perhaps even their ways of knowing via connectedness with ancestors, heritage, and family have been diminished.

INTERMARRIAGE

The most poignant realm of battering forces for the Jewish family is associated with intermarriage. Intermarriages are now almost a normative state of the battered Jewish family. Work with numerous intermarried families in various agencies and private settings has evidenced marriages which commenced with declarations of love and minimal thought as to the nuances, nuisances, and nascence of problems and issues related to intermarriage. Some met rocky roads early on with the planning of wedding ceremonies, choices of clergy, types of related customs and ceremonies, etc. Others ran into the proverbial in-law problems.

But most began to reel around the birth of their children, at which time circumcision versus baptism, naming versus christening, other traditional rites and customs became grist for the mill of decision making. Shortly thereafter, the greatest decisions began to hang heavily; i.e., with which values shall we inculcate our children, and what sort of educational choices shall we make? Great differences in past, present, and future investments came to light. Added to these conundrums were the divided loyalties, requests, and demands felt by children and by grandparents, yielding a situation that was compounded, and often confounded.

In the 1992 *American Jewish Yearbook*, there is an important study regarding the Jewish identity of participants in intermarriages.[12] A total of 197,078 households were studied. These represented a total Jewish population in the eight U.S. communities studied of over 433,104 individuals in in-married households, 35,266 in conversionary households, and 106,163 individuals in mixed-married households. All told, 574,533 individuals, or about 9.75 percent of American Jewry, were included in the study—quite a sizable sampling. The study found that, although intermarriage rates varied widely by community, there was a common pattern of sharply rising rates of over 50 percent among the younger age cohorts.

For every couple consisting of two Jewish partners, there were approximately two new couples in which only one of the partners was Jewish. The magnitude of the change in rates of intermarriage is embodied in the shocking statistic that among those marrying before 1965, five times as many Jewish marriages were homogamous as opposed to mixed marriages—a truly significant difference. According to this Brandeis study, mixed-married families—where the non-Jewish partner did not convert—were far less likely to identify Jewishly than families where the non-Jew converted. Unfortunately, however, conversion rates dropped just as intermarriage rates were rising. According to the authors of this study:

> Overall, the chances of a mixed marriage resulting in a single-identity household at any level of Jewish identification are extremely slim, and the chances of it resulting in a single-identity household at a high level of Jewish identification are infinitesimal. Under these circumstances, the likelihood of creating an unambiguous Jewish identity, should such be the intention or desire, is virtually nil.[13]

One of the greatest concerns regarding the demographic implications of such high rates of mixed marriages is, of course, the Jewish identity of the children of such marriages. A total of 644,000 children under eighteen years of age were living in households identified as mixed-married in the National Jewish Population Study of 1990. Of these children only 25 percent were being raised as Jews at the time of the survey; 45 percent were being raised in another religion; and 30 percent were being raised without any religion. According to Professor Sidney Goldstein, in his "Profile of American Jewry":

> Unless a large majority of the latter (i.e. those raised without any religion), opt to be identified as Jews when they reach adulthood, most children of mixed marriages will be lost to Judaism; they will be Jews by descent only, either through the maternal or paternal line. These potential losses, continues Dr. Goldstein, constitute a major challenge to the Jewish community.[14]

Given that the Jewish community at large, and the synagogues in particular, have done little thus far to reach out to intermarried couples, and even less in terms of reaching out educationally to their children, this nexus, or "convergence zone," spells disaster to those battered Jewish families whose identity and group membership was once assured and secure.

Kurt Lewin summed up the psychological importance of the individual's group membership as "the ground on which he stands, which gives or denies him social status, gives or denies him security and help. The firmness of the physical ground on which we tread is not always thought of. Dynamically, however, the firmness and clearness of his ground determines what the individual wishes to do, what he can do, and how he will do it."[15]

Put differently, Victor Sanua referred to Sherif's description of identification as a process in which the individual's "self-identity becomes related to a group, and in which his experiences and actions are profoundly affected by his relationship with the group by his conceiving himself as part of it and experiencing its triumphs and vicissitudes as joys and tribulations."[16] This all will depend upon how Jews perceive themselves and their connectedness to their group. According to Georg Simmel, the individual "receives" certain "constituent elements" which he develops, and then expresses and returns, in his choices of affiliations with social groups.[17] The important notion here is that one's choices, attitudes, and participation regarding affiliation with social groups is directly related to what one has "received." What future groups of Jewish children will "receive" remains an unknown.

Simmel went on to describe the conflict-laden process of the addition of multiple reference groups and roles for the individual. He anticipated that:

> As the individual leaves his established position within one primary group, he comes to stand at a point at which many groups "intersect." The individual as a moral personality comes to be circumscribed in an entirely new way, but he also faces new problems. The security and lack of ambiguity in his former position gives way to uncertainty in the conditions of his life. . . . It may come to pass, external and internal conflicts arising through the multiplicity of group-affiliations will threaten the individual with psychological tensions or even a schizophrenic break.[18]

These individuals will perforce need to develop new strategies to negotiate the new situations in which they find themselves.

TWO CASE EXAMPLES

Case 1

The battered Jewish family is embodied in the case of domestic abuse and violence in the home of two Jewish lawyers who were married for eighteen years. They were proud of their Jewish home, and sent their three children to the best Jewish day schools. Differences emerged between them and their children as choices of high schools needed to be made. The children maintained that only "out of town" high schools would meet their enhanced religious learning needs, whereas the parents were staunchly dedicated to the pursuit of the finest secular education available.

It became clear almost from the outset that significant tensions prevailed between the spouses. Although they boasted that they held consonant views on most major issues in their lives, the competitive bickering and denigration of one another over minute details was so preeminent that it overshadowed even the major ongoing self-deprecation and continual obsessional behavior of the husband.

Since meetings with both spouses disintegrated into shouting matches, I began meeting with each spouse individually. In their individual sessions, each began to reveal "secrets" of their respective lives and of their marriage. Mr. D. revealed that his father always "cut him down," and that his mother always listened to his father and was depressed most of the time. Moreover, Mr. D. revealed that in no way could he compete with his wife, whose law practice was thriving whilst his was literally on the verge of collapse. Mrs. D. confirmed all of this, and added that Mr. D. was impotent.

Most importantly, Mrs. D. reported that Mr. D. was erupting not only with his usual uncontained verbal rage, but also with physical violence. Very shortly thereafter, Mrs. D. appeared with bruises all over her neck, arms, and legs. Mr. D. had tried to choke her in a fit of rage, but she would not involve police. She realized, however, that she could no longer go on as she had, "covering for him" for all these years in the community, at synagogue, work, and the like.

Although neither spouse made the connection, they announced that Mr. D.'s father had recently passed away. When Mr. D. saw the incredible black-and-blue marks on his wife, and was made aware that she had shown them to others, he followed up with a very serious suicide attempt that landed him in intensive care, and then in a psychiatric hospital for two months. A separation and then divorce ensued, and all three children have wound up wounded and "out of town," at the Jewish high schools of their choice.

Discussion. This case evidences a "convergence zone"—a concept emanating from modern neuroscience that deals with mapping out different zones of the mind[19]—of battering forces upon the Jewish family, including mental illness spanning at least two generations, i.e., depression, obsessional behavior, elements of paranoia, and psychological and physical impotence, along with the breakdown of high-powered careers, with great financial, social, and personal devastation. Literal, actual mental and physical battering ensued, along with the breakup of a family and its dispersion over numerous states. What had been externally perceived as a model, successful Jewish family was now broken apart into individuals flailing about to stay afloat.

Battering conflicts of secular education goals espoused by the parents in the family went head to head with the children's particular notion of what they thought they needed for their own strictly religious needs. The children continued moving toward more and more "rightist" positions based on their connection with groups other than their family. The family's own traditions and "ways of knowing" were devalued and discarded by the children. A sense of internal battering was acute, as the family could no longer rely on its own markers of tradition, which had been normative for at least the past five generations by the parents' reportage. In addition, the family had little ability to negotiate differences together, and to participate in joint decision-making processes. It was as if they could not deal with, or ward off, all the internal and external battering forces.

Case 2

Yet another "pattern of intersection," or convergence zone, of battering comes together in the following case, which depicts the making of a shattered union and shattered family, along with a look at a particular brand of "in-marriage" specific to the Jewish people. This is not a case of intermarriage, but contains some elements of the issues cited in the section on intermarriage above.

Judy made aliyah to a kibbutz in Israel against her parents' wishes, and to forsake her middle-class, materialistic past, by her description. Within the year she married a "true-blue kib-butznik" and surrendered all her possessions to the collectivity of the kibbutz, including her prized stereo system. Her husband, Rami, had grown up on the kibbutz after his mother suffered a psychotic break and was permanently institutionalized, and his father abandoned him as he was no longer able to care for him. Rami was eight years old at the time, and to date wracking sobs emanate from his core being at the mere recollection of any events connected to that time of his life.

After a year of married life in the kibbutz setting, the couple decided to strike out on their own in Tel Aviv. As farming skills were not in great demand in this urban center, Rami was rele-gated to ditch digging on road-construction projects, and Judy, disgusted with doing menial labor, decided to begin a family. Her pregnancy was unremarkable until a bout with a protracted labor and an unattended delivery because, so Judy claimed, the nurses did not believe that the baby was coming when she screamed to them that it was. Instead she was instructed not to push, and to hold her legs together.

A beautiful baby boy, however, soon emerged, but not before turning blue from lack of oxygen. His limbs were flaccid, his muscle tone poor, and his prognosis, according to the doctors, was "that of a vegetable." Immediate institutionalization of the child was recommended, but the mother persisted, resisting sub-stantial pressure, and took the child home from hospital. Rami connected with the child but agreed with the doctors that place-ment was the best alternative. Judy fought on, and made the rounds to medical doctors, rehabilitation facilities, and "anyone who would listen, and might offer any advice." Against incredible odds, she kept the child at home, and dealt with him to the best of her ability.

The diagnosis of cerebral palsy was made along with mental retardation. Judy was convinced that her son was bright and could be responsive. Without her husband's support, she carried him about and attempted to train him. When even bread became hard to come by, the family picked up and flew back to the States, courtesy of Judy's parents. Ten years of assorted odd jobs and financial hard times ensued, but at least Judy felt that she was doing the best she could for Dror, along with her two other children. With a major malpractice suit underway against the medical group that did not deliver Dror in a timely fashion, Judy and Rami took out loans and built a new home that suited Dror's special accessibility and wheelchair needs.

In the meantime, Judy felt lonely, emotionally unsupported, and overwhelmed by household and childcare duties. Her husband continued to work very long hours, and was unavailable emotionally, especially at the critical juncture for Judy when her father was sick and dying. Another man, who worked at Rami's office, did some household repairs and befriended her. Under Rami's nose, this relationship flourished unbeknownst to him. Judy and John became more brazen about their involvement, almost flaunting their relationship, but it took some two years before Rami caught on and objected to Judy's involvement with this "non-Jew." To Rami this was a great blow, considering that from his point of view he had dedicated all his efforts and finances to his family and in particular to Dror's benefit, and was now being supplanted by a man who was being touted as a great "support."

When Judy announced that she would be moving out, Rami became immobilized, severely depressed, and threatened suicide. The children were torn apart, knowing that optimally Dror needed to be in the house that had been specially built for him, and yet their mother, their psychological parent, would be moving away. Significant acting-out behavior became manifest in their schools as well as at home. But Judy moved out. She said she needed her space, and took along the two younger children, finally admitting what a burden Dror had become to her. Rami decompensated, and could no longer work. Neither could he care for Dror. The house that had been built for Dror could no longer house him. His behavior deteriorated, and the many gains he had consolidated throughout his lifetime, including skills garnered in preparation for a lavish Bar Mitzvah celebration, went down the tubes in fits of rage and increasingly erratic behaviors. The institution he was spared from at birth became his sole option for life. A nasty divorce followed, and the two other children scorned both their parents, and the non-Jewish man who had linked up with their mother.

Discussion. In looking at the case, it becomes apparent that a gulf existed in the "in-marriage" between Israeli husband and American-born wife. Anecdotally reported statistics indicate high divorce rates among such couples, and clear cultural and sometimes religious and/or value gaps extant between them. Of course, not all such marriages include the additional battering force of the tragic, constant mourning produced by giving birth to a child with so many deficits, ultimately affecting the entire family. This is the key battering force in this case. And then there was the child who is now the parent, who had been abandoned at an early age, who was now once again abandoned by the female figure in his life.[20] Moreover, his own need for institutionalization as a child was now revisited with the need to institutionalize his own son. The Hebrew language he cherished was discarded by his wife and children, and he felt that he himself was discarded. The Jewish traditions and Sabbaths and holidays that had anchored their lives were usurped by Christian holidays that had never before been celebrated. All of these constituted external and internal battering forces for this family. Culture shock of vast proportions pervaded.[21]

CONCLUSION

In conclusion, it comes as no surprise that families such as those depicted above, who were connected to history and tradition, suddenly visualized themselves as isolated units whose sole preoccupation became survival.[22] This led to phenomena of "me-centeredness," and a fostering of the individual's needs, wants, desires, above all. These are not traditional Jewish ways of knowing and certainly not of living; hence major life-event struggles ensued and continued to unfold. Internal battering became coupled with, and compounded by, external web-of-life battering. The coincidence of the two becomes too much to bear, and it is this nexus of the confluence of battering that leaves the Jewish family besieged and in crisis.

REFERENCES

1. C. H. Kempe and R. E. Helfer, eds., *The Battered Child*, 3rd ed. (Chicago: University of Chicago Press, 1980). See also James Garbaimo et al., *The Psychologically Battered Child* (San Francisco: Jossey-Bass, 1986).

2. See Barrie Thorne and Marilyn Yalom, eds., *Rethinking the Family* (New York: Longman, 1982); Paul Pearsall, *Power of the Family* (New York: Bantam, 1990); Faye J. Crosby, *Juggling* (New York: Free Press, 1991); Steven Carter and Julia Sokol, *Lives Without Balance* (New York: Villard Books, 1992); Christopher Lasch, *Haven in a Heartless World: The Family Besieged* (New York: Basic Books, 1977).

3. Gilbert S. Rosenthal, *The Jewish Family in a Changing World* (New York: Yoseloff, 1970); Norman Linzer, *The Jewish Family* (New York: Federation of Jewish Philanthropies, 1972); idem, "The Jewish Family," in *The Nature of Man in Judaism and Social Work* (New York: Federation of Jewish Philanthropies, 1978); Norman Linzer, ed., *Judaism and Mental Health* (New York: Board of Jewish Education, 1978); Moshe Halevi Spero, *Judaism and Psychology: Halakhic Perspectives* (New York: Ktav/Yeshiva University Press, 1981); *Journal of Judaism and Psychology*, 1984–1992; Chaim Waxman, "How Many Are We? Where Are We Going?" *Jewish Life* 6, no. 1 (Spring–Summer 1982): 37–44; Reuven P. Bulka, *Individual, Family, Community: Judeo-Psychological Perspectives* (Oakville, Ont.: Mosaic Press, 1989).

4. See Thomas W. Miller, ed., *Stressful Life Events* (Madison, Conn.: International Universities Press, 1989).

5. R. A. Pruchno, F. C. Blow, and M. S. Smyer, "Life Events and Interdependent Lives: Implications for Research & Intervention," *Human Development* 27 (1984): 31–41.

6. G. O. Hagestad, "Problems & Promises in the Social Psychology of Intergenerational Relations," in *Stability and Change in the Family*, ed. J. Fogel,

W. Hatfield, V. Kiegler, and R. M. March (New York: Academic Press, 1981), pp. 211–218.

7. Steven J. Wolin and Linda A. Bennett, "Issues on Family Identity," *Family Process* 23 (September 1984): 401–420.

8. Martin Buber, I and Thou (New York: Charles Scribner's Sons, 1958).

9. See Lyn Mikel Breson and Carol Gilligan, *Meeting at the Crossroads: Women's Psychology & Girls' Development* (Cambridge, Mass.: Harvard University Press, 1992); Mary Field Belenky et al., *Women's Ways of Knowing: The Development of Self, Voice & Mind* (New York: Basic Books, 1986).

10. Belenky, *Women's Ways of Knowing*, chaps. 4 and 5.

11. Rivka Ausubel Danzig, "Marginality: Orthodox Jewish Students in Social Work Education" (Ph.D. diss., Yeshiva University, 1981).

12. Peter Y. Medding et al., "Jewish Identity in Conversionary and Mixed Marriages," *American Jewish Year Book*, vol. 91 (New York: American Jewish Committee, 1992), pp. 3–76.

13. Ibid., p. 39.

14. Ibid., p. 127.

15. Kurt Lewin, *Resolving Social Conflicts* (New York: Harper, 1948), p. 174.

16. Victor Sanua, "Patterns of Identification with the Jewish Community in the USA," *Jewish Journal of Sociology* 6, no. 2, p. 47.

17. Georg Simmel, *The Web of Group Affiliations* (Glencoe, Ill.: Free Press, 1964).

18. Ibid., p. 141.

19. June Kinoshita, "Mapping of the Mind," *New York Times Magazine*, October 18, 1992.

20. See James Garbarino, Edna Guttmann, and Janis Wilson Seeley, *The Psychologically Battered Child* (New York: Jossey-Bass, 1986).

21. See Peter L. Berger, *Invitation to Sociology: A Humanistic Perspective* (New York: Doubleday, 1963).

22. See Frank M. Loewenberg, *Religion and Social Work Practice in Contemporary American Society* (New York: Columbia University Press, 1988).

CHANGING ROLES OF JEWISH WOMEN

Francine Klagsbrun

"So," my father says, his voice slurry as a result of a stroke suffered some twenty years ago, "in another year Sarah will be twenty-four, right?"

"Right, Daddy," I reply, "but at the moment she's just twenty-three."

"Those years go by quickly," he retorts. The stroke never dulled the sharpness of his mind. Nor, having turned ninety-seven recently, has my father ever hesitated to say what is on that mind. Clearly, the subject of concern for him at the moment is my daughter Sarah.

"She should be thinking about marriage soon."

"When she's ready to think about it, she'll think about it," I answer, barely concealing my irritation. Currently my daughter is completing a post-baccalaureate program of pre-med courses she had not taken in college and applying to medical schools. It's not that marriage isn't there someplace in her mind, but for now it's not her highest priority. Passing organic chemistry is.

"What does she need such a hard life for?" he continues, as though oblivious of my angry tone. "Everything has changed so much. She's a lovely young woman. What she should be doing now is getting married, settling down . . ."

"Tell me about your grandmother," I interrupt him. "I was looking at that old picture of her again just the other day." Stirring up the past is always a surefire way of moving away from a subject I don't feel like discussing with my father.

"Oh, my grandmother," he says, settling comfortably into his chair. "You know, she was ninety-five years old when that picture was taken, and still climbing the five flights to our flat on the Lower East Side."

I know that. I've heard it many times. "And in Russia?" I ask.

"In Russia, before we came here, she was known throughout our village. She was an educated woman. She could read Hebrew as well as Yiddish. But she also worked very hard. Her husband died when my father was a young boy. She managed to raise her children by selling this and that in the marketplace. When my father married, she came to live with him and my mother. She grew all the fruits and vegetables the family ate, in the garden outside our home. She also took care of the children most of the time because my mother was so busy working."

"I didn't know Bubbi worked. What kind of work did she do?"

Again, I know the answer, but I like to hear it from him. My grandmother took in boarders in the house in which she lived with her husband, five sons, and mother-in-law. She cooked for them and washed their clothes, enhancing the family income in that way. In her "spare" time, she helped her husband sell tobacco and salt in the nearby town.

"Of course, she wasn't the only woman who worked hard," my father says, after retelling my grandmother's story. "There were others whose husbands were scholars and studied all day while their wives worked and supported their families."

"I know," I answer, smiling. "Now what were you saying about Sarah getting married, settling down, and not working so hard? That doesn't seem to be the tradition for women in our family, or many other Jewish ones like ours. Maybe, after all, things haven't changed quite as much as you like to think they have."

The changing roles of the Jewish woman? Of course there have been enormous changes in women's roles in the past two decades or so, and of course the impact of those changes on the family has been far-reaching. But as we launch into our examination of change, let's not forget that the Jewish woman of today is not a total anomaly. She does not come out of nowhere. The roles many Jewish women have been taking on in recent years have their roots in roles many earlier Jewish women played. My father's grandmother, my great-grandmother, was—to use today's terminology—a single parent of four sons and a daughter. She worked to support them, with no help at all from her husband's family, and saw to it that the sons, at least, were all Jewishly educated. My grandmother was a working mother, always trying to juggle her time between her children and her boarders, her household chores and her merchanting chores. There were many Jewish women like her in Europe, and many others among the immigrants to America.[1] We have a tradition for women holding many roles within their families—mothers and housewives, but also wage earners—and we need to reach back into that tradition as we try to find our way in our often-confusing modern world.

One of the reasons we tend to forget the connections between today's Jewish women and women of the past is that we often contrast our contemporary situation with what immediately preceded it. We compare the past twenty years to the twenty years before them, and they seem centuries apart. Many of the changes in women's roles and attitudes toward themselves and their families began in the late 1960s and early 1970s. The previous decade, the 1950s, when I came of age and later married, was the most domestic of times. Earlier, during the 1940s, women took over jobs in factories and offices as men marched off to war. When the troops returned the women were pushed out of those jobs and the wartime image of "Rosie the Riveter" working in the steel plant was replaced by the soft, sexy, kittenish woman who wanted nothing more than to please her man, and, once married, to devote herself full-time to her family. That wish became the all-around ideal of the 1950s.

For Jewish women, the full-time Mom had been establishing herself as the norm even before the war years. As Jewish immigrant men built businesses and became financially secure, they turned away from their old shtetl attitudes.[2] It was a mark of pride for a man to be able to support his family with no help from his wife. It was a mark of pride to be able to provide her with beautiful clothes, to pamper and baby her.

My mother once told me that in the years when my father was establishing a business, he worked practically around the clock and was often out of town. She would have loved to go back to the work she had done as a bookkeeper before they married, at least part-time, but she worried, she said, that "people would talk about us." So she stayed home, alone at first, and later, alone with her children. My father never made it as the big businessman he would have liked to be, and we rarely had household help. My mother was grateful, she said, that she could keep busy caring for her home and family. Other women she knew, with little else to do, spent almost all of their time shopping.

By the 1950s, the postwar woman, and in Jewish life, the post-shtetl woman, was a full-time homemaker. Parents like mine sent their daughters as well as their sons to college, even graduate school, and expected them equally to bring home good grades and honors. But the unspoken understanding was that for the daughters the degrees and honors were ornaments. Real life was about marriage and children. And if male Jewish writers poked fun at overprotective Jewish mothers or overadorned Jewish princesses—creating images, by the way, that still haunt and hurt us—in real life, those self-sacrificing mothers and their educated, family-devoted daughters were (and in some ways still are) community ideals.[3]

Against this background of the late forties, fifties, and early sixties, the feminist revolution of the late sixties and the seventies appears overwhelming, seemingly undoing everything that had come before it. But, in fact, there had been other "befores." There had been my grandmother and great-grandmother, and long before them the seventeenth-century Jewish woman Glueckel of Hameln, who ran successful business ventures even while she reared her twelve orphaned children.[4] And long before her was the biblical woman of valor, who bought fields and planted vineyards and sold her handmade linen garments to local merchants.[5] So, when we speak about the changing roles of Jewish women or—as the present lecture series is called—the crises in the family, we need to think not about one kind of Jewish woman, but about the many roles Jewish women have played throughout history, and not about only one kind of Jewish family, but about the many strands that have made up the Jewish family over time. If we think that way, we may find that we are not as disassociated from our past as we sometimes believe we are.

For all our connection to the past, indeed, the feminist revolution of the last twenty years is a true revolution that has altered forever the position of women in society. While we must not forget that we have antecedents in history, we must also recognize that in many ways the situation of women today, including Jewish women, is radically different from what it was in earlier years. The radicalism comes not in the facts of women working or not working, marrying or not marrying, but in the changed perspectives women have toward themselves and that men have begun to have toward women. Never before in modern history have women as a group seen themselves as capable of determining their own life paths, of making choices, of leaving their mark on the world not only within but also outside their families.

Every day in the newspapers you see stories about women breaking new ground—whether it's holding the office of attorney general or opening their own funeral parlors. We have moved so far beyond the sixties and seventies, when it all began, that many young women today speak of postfeminism, or no feminism at all.[6] They so take it for granted that women can hold any role they want to in society—that my daughter will enter medical school, that her women friends will be social workers and lawyers, filmmakers or rabbis—that they no longer regard these as feminist achievements. My grandmother and great-grandmother struggled with many issues women today struggle with in terms of their homes and children, but where we differ now from generations of women who came before us is in our attitude that women and men have equal opportunities, equal options, and equal control over their lives.

Now, that attitude has had a profound effect on the family not only because women have always been central to family life but because family life itself has changed over the decades. When my father's mother was busy cooking or cleaning for her boarders, or working alongside her husband, my father and his brothers knew that their grandmother was around to care for them, as were other grandmothers for other grandchildren.

Don't misunderstand. The idea that Jewish families of the past, or any families, lived together in large, extended-family units is a myth that recent social historians have proved untrue.[7] In every age and society, they have shown, people lived in nuclear units, not in large, multifamily ones. But we, in our society, have carried the nuclear family to its extreme. We not only don't live in homes with grandparents, we often don't live near grandparents or other relatives. So when both parents are working, few family members are available to fill in the gaps. My father, also, had four siblings he could turn to for companionship and comfort. In today's small families, people rarely have more than one sibling—if that—to depend on. Given the narrowing of the family, then—the lack of relatives close by and the small numbers within—the new roles women have assumed have had a special impact. And that impact is strongly felt in the Jewish community.

Let's look at it. First, there is the matter of numbers. As women like my daughter prepare to enter professions, they postpone marriage and then childbearing. Ironically, one study has shown that among Jews, unlike Protestants or Catholics, the more educated a couple, the greater the number of children they expect to have. Jews with doctorates, for example, expect to have 2.2 children, whereas Jews with only a college degree expect only 1.8 children. In reality, however, just the opposite occurs. Jewish couples have fewer children than they expect to have, and as education increases, the proportion of couples with no children also increases.[8] My daughter, for example, says she wants to have three or four children. She also says she will not marry until she completes at least her first two years of medical school. At that time she will be twenty-six. If she waits to complete all her medical schooling before having her first child, she will be twenty-eight or older. That means the next child will be born when she is in her thirties. Will there be time for a third child? A fourth? Will she still want them?

In addition, and tragically, women who postpone childbearing until they are in their thirties or forties often suffer from unwanted infertility. In general, Jewish women are less likely than women of any other religious or ethnic group to say that they wish to remain childless.[9] So infertility can be extremely painful for them, and it is not surprising that in the 1990 Jewish Population Survey, conducted by the Council of Jewish Federations, a relatively large number—165,000 couples—said that at one time or another they had sought assistance with adoption.[10]

Given the high level of education of Jewish women and their postponement of marriage and parenthood, the overall Jewish birthrate has long been among the lowest of any religious or ethnic group. The exceptions are Hasidim and other Orthodox groups, the only ones who have children above replacement level, meaning at least 2.1 children per family.[11] These low numbers have brought on an outcry from rabbis and community leaders, a worry that the Jewish family will dwindle away to nothing as the years go on, and that Jews will become an insignificant minority in the United States. To be honest, I don't find myself shaking with that kind of anxiety. Yes, it would be good for Jewish families to have more children and for the size of the community to constantly grow. But the threat to our community comes more from intermarriage and from assimilation than from low birthrates. Only the Jewishly educated and Jewishly committed will perpetuate Judaism, and it is the job of community leaders and others to push as hard as possible for such education rather than constantly bemoan the low birthrate. As far as political clout is concerned, our numbers may be small, but as Jewish women as well as men achieve positions of prominence in the broader commumty, Jews will continue to exert influence out of proportion to their numbers.

In any event, whether or not we wish for higher fertility rates, Jewish women, like other American women, are postponing marriage and children while they prepare for careers and occupations. And like other women they are entering the work force in unprecedented numbers. In 1991, for example, 58 percent of women with children under six were in the labor force, most of them working full time. In 1960, just 20 percent of women with children under six worked outside their homes.[12] The numbers are lower in the Jewish community, but they follow a similar pattern. Sociologist Steven M. Cohen, studying Jews in large metropolitan areas during the early 1980s, found that about half of Jewish women with young children worked outside their homes, a quarter of them full-time and a quarter part-time.[13] A later study, in 1988, found that in many cities about two-thirds of Jewish women with children under six were in the labor force, either full-or part-time.[14]

What effect have these high numbers had on the quality of family life? On a positive note, the numbers of working women and the acceptance by society of the changing roles of women have led men to assume more responsibilities than they ever had before for childrearing and home care. Far more than their fathers, or even their older brothers, young men today expect to be involved in changing diapers and helping with homework, and enjoy doing so.

The bad news is that women still carry the ultimate responsibility for all that happens in the home, no matter how many hours a woman works or how high-powered her position. In her study of working mothers, sociologist Arlie Hochschild uses the term "second shift" to characterize women's work at home.[15] Women work all day at their paid jobs, she says, and then they work an unpaid second shift at home, cleaning, cooking, caring for children, in the traditional roles women always had. In fact, the term "changing roles" of women is in many ways misleading. In the burdens of their lives, working women today are not so different from my grandmother and great-grandmother. They have taken on additional roles outside their homes, but still hold the old ones within. This lack of change in domestic responsibilities is the problem of working women today.

It is a problem that will be brought home to many of you, perhaps in your own lives, and also when you see clients in practice. There are women who hold excellent positions, have lovely children and good marital relations, but see themselves as failures. Why? Because they cannot be the perfect mothers, perfect wives, and perfect workers or executives they are trying to be.

In the Jewish community, the stresses can be especially potent, particularly for those women who are Jewishly committed and who want to transmit that commitment to their children. Torn between their work and their families, always trying to juggle their time, they sense in many cases disapproval by community leaders, an attitude that the Jewish family is in crisis and they are to blame for having taken on new roles.[16]

The fact is, however, that at no time in Jewish history has the Jewish woman, as involved as she may have been in the care of her children, assumed full responsibility for transmitting Jewish values and culture to them. More important, at no time has the Jewish family sustained itself. "The family today is asked to do things which it can't possibly do," wrote the late Gerson D. Cohen, chancellor of the Jewish Theological Seminary. "It is called upon to replace community, to provide leisure, love, respect, satisfaction, fulfillment. But that's impossible, because we can't do these things in isolation. We can do them only as a community."[17]

The Jewish community today agonizes over the lower Jewish birthrate, the numbers of Jewish working wives, the stress on the family, yet—ultimately—it does not do nearly enough to help the family or the community itself. One of the most crucial, most obvious, ways to help is with good Jewish child-care programs. The recent ruckus about Zoe Baird and Kimba Wood and illegal aliens has brought home to Americans at large the crisis in child care that plagues this nation. The crisis is even worse in the Jewish community because we are missing a vital opportunity not only to help families but to educate children into Jewish life.

As things stand now, working Jewish parents hire nannies or babysitters for their children in a dizzying, catch-as-catch-can system that depends on individual resources, contacts, and luck. The women hired often speak little English, and certainly have no Jewish knowledge. How much more meaningful it would be for a child to be cared for within a Jewish environment by people trained to impart Jewish tradition even as they offer care and nurturing. Synagogues could offer child-care programs—as many churches do. They could charge sliding rates, depending on income. On a larger scale, community organizations and agencies should develop a variety of programs or, at the very least, think through the child-care needs of the community and make concrete recommendations.[18]

Is it better for a child to be cared for by a loving parent than in a day-care program? Probably yes, although the case has been made that children learn greater flexibility when they spend time with other children and caretakers. Is it better for a parent to work part-time during a child's early years of life rather than full-time? Probably yes. But these statements hold true for fathers as well as mothers. And the reality is that in many families neither father nor mother can afford to work only part-time, both for financial reasons and because most careers demand full-time work. Nor have most businesses and industries provided the kind of flex time that would benefit working parents. Nor, I might add, have Jewish agencies and organizations taken steps to ease the burdens of working parents in their own midst. So instead of castigating women for working or haranguing them to have more children, it would be useful for Jewish leaders to face the realities and plan intelligent solutions for them. High on the list of planning should be child-care programs.

· The lack of reality with which the Jewish community has greeted the fact of working mothers is reflected also in attitudes toward other changes in the family. Foremost among them is the preponderance of single-parent homes today. There were plenty of single parents like my great-grandmother in earlier days, only then they were called widows because their status resulted mostly from the death of their spouses. As difficult as their lives were— and they were difficult—they had a place within the Jewish community. They were the subject of biblical injunctions admonishing the people to care for the widows and orphans among them, and often regarded as the responsibility of the community.

In the United States, it was not until the 1970s that more single-parent homes and more stepfamilies were formed because of divorce than of death.[19] During the seventies and eighties the divorce rate in the United States soared to heights never before reached, to the point at which, one of every two marriages contracted will end in divorce or has already done so. In 1991, a quarter of all U.S. children under the age of eighteen lived in single-parent homes, most of them with their mothers.[20] Divorce figures have leveled off, but at a high rate, so we can expect a continuation of large numbers of divorces and single-parent families well into the nineties.

The figures are somewhat more moderate in the Jewish community, but have increased greatly in the last twenty years. In Boston, for example, the divorce rate among Jews in 1985 was five times higher than it had been in 1965.[21] In the Jewish community, also, unlike other ethnic groups, only a small number of single parents are unwed mothers, and those few are usually women in their thirties or forties who have chosen not to marry but to raise children on their own.

Has the increase in divorce and single-parent homes resulted from the changing roles of women? To some extent, yes. The stresses of dual-career marriages, including the lack of time husbands and wives have to spend with each other, contribute to divorce. Moreover, as women have become more economically independent than ever before, they have felt freer to leave unsatisfactory marriages and strike out on their own. But most divorces are more complex than that and cannot simply be "blamed" on women's increased independence. For one thing, equality between husband and wife often strengthens marriage, not weakens it. For another, the openness ushered in by the sixties and seventies made divorce easy to obtain, and the lack of stigma attached to it has added to the ease. Even among the Orthodox, who have the lowest divorce rates in the Jewish community, the rates are considerably higher today than they were fifty years ago. Among the Orthodox, incidentally, the numbers of agunoth, women whose husbands refuse to give them a Jewish divorce, have grown and the problem has become particularly pressing in recent years.[22]

Generally women and children suffer most from divorce. Judith Wallerstein, who has studied divorced families over the course of years, has shown that its effects on children can last far into adulthood.[23] For single parents who have custody of their children—usually mothers—the financial pressures can be devastating. In Steven Cohen's study of Jewish families in major metropolitan areas, most single mothers, unlike married ones, worked full-time, and only a small number worked part-time. In terms of Jewish income distribution, writes Cohen, single mothers are, as a group, living in relative poverty.[24] And a 1987 study of the Jewish community of Rochester, New York, found that over half the divorced women—many of them single mothers—

made less than $20,000 a year, but none of the divorced men made less than $30,000 a year.[25]

Ironically, often the women who lead the most traditional lives during marriage suffer the most after a divorce. Women who did not work at all or limited their work to part-time while married may find themselves with little source of income and few skills afterward. Many of them feel betrayed not by the women's movement but by the traditional values they bought into in the belief that marriage is forever.

In addition to their financial suffering, single-parent families often suffer from an overcloseness or overdependence among family members. Out of their own loneliness and need, single mothers may make their children their buddies, confiding in them more than they should or pushing them to take on more adult responsibilities than they are ready for. Social workers dealing with single-parent families need to help parents establish boundaries between themselves and their children and to recognize the children's own sense of loss and need to be parented.[26]

With all their difficulties, many divorced women say that they and their children feel unwelcome in traditional Jewish communal settings. Rabbis and community leaders, eager to encourage stable, two-parent homes, tend to ignore the special needs of the divorced, both women and men. But, with higher incomes, men are more often able to maintain their ties to their synagogue or community organizations, while their former wives as well as children simply drift away.

The fact is that making single parents and their children feel welcome within the community can enhance the community by keeping those divorced families, and particularly the children, involved and Jewishly committed. Today's single-parent families are yesterday's widows and orphans, and community concern and care needs to be extended to them in the same way.

To recap for a moment: The new roles Jewish women have assumed outside their families have opened up worlds of occupa-

tions and professions for them but have also opened up new family problems—lower fertility rates, the stresses of trying to
balance work and family life, pressures on marriage, and the pain
of divorce and single-parent homes. All of these issues call for
sensitivity and creativity on the part of Jewish agencies and organizations.

But the problems are only one aspect of the sweeping changes
that have accompanied women's new roles. Other aspects are
more subtle, less quantifiable, yet as real, as significant, and perhaps even more long-lasting. They concern the strength, the
power, and the knowledge women have acquired as they have
assumed their new roles.

Let's take a dark area of family life: domestic violence—abuse
of wives, and often of children, by husbands. For years society
ignored wife-beatings. The police would advise wives who dared
complain to make the best of their situation, and send them right
back home to their abusive husbands. In the Jewish community,
the idea that a husband would beat his wife was so anathema that
nobody dared speak of it, not even social service professionals.[27]
We do not know the exact numbers of such situations, but we
know now that they exist, in all segments of Jewish society as of
non-Jewish. We know because women, and many of them
Orthodox women, have established battered women's shelters
scattered throughout their communities. We also know because
Jewish women trained as lawyers have taken up the cause of battered women and brought it to public attention. Women, in their
new roles, have made it possible for other women to say "No
more," and to change their lives and those of their children.

On a much brighter note, among the many new roles women
have assumed in the Jewish community are roles of scholarship.
For ages, women were kept out of the scholarly study of Judaism.
In the shtetls of Eastern Europe, as my father noted, there were
men who studied all day while their wives supported them, but
the wives themselves were generally unlearned. My great-grand-

mother was unique among the women of her town because she could read Hebrew as well as Yiddish. Most women could read only Yiddish, if even that. Even after yeshivot for women—the Beis Yaakov schools—opened in the early twentieth century, first in Europe and later in America, and until fairly recent times, few women received extensive Jewish educations, and fewer still learned to study Talmud.[28] That has all changed now. Girls in many Orthodox and Conservative day schools study Talmud on an equal level with boys. More exciting, in the Orthodox movement in particular, groups of adult women of all ages are studying Talmud and other sacred texts in the tradition of the men of the yeshivot. Some of these women will become teachers of others over time. But more important for our discussion, all of these women will be able to teach their children, their sons and daughters, the classic texts of Judaism. Traditionally women have been seen as the moral forces within the family, whereas fathers had responsibility for the actual education of their children—their sons, that is, not their daughters.[29] But what better way to strengthen the Jewish family than to have knowledgeable mothers who impart their love of that knowledge to all their children?

For the most part, fewer Conservative and Reform women join groups engaged in serious study of the Talmud and other texts. But those movements ordain women as rabbis, giving them major religious-leadership positions. Through their work they serve as models for young women in their communities. The message they convey is that there is a place for women in Judaism, not only in the home but at the center of community life. Their visibility helps firm the ties of women to their tradition, and those firmer ties can only help the family.

Ultimately, the active role many women take in prayer services also enhances Jewish family life. My daughter, a graduate of a Jewish day school, reads from the Torah, chants the Haftarah, and leads services both in her havura group and in the Conservative synagogue to which we belong in New York. She has told me many times that her sense of belonging because of those activities is a major factor in her determination to marry someone as Jewishly knowledgeable and able as she and to make sure that her children have the same knowledge and commitment as she does.

One of the most remarkable changes, along these lines, has, again, come in the Orthodox movement. Because women are not permitted to lead services with men or be counted in a minyan, a quorum of ten men, women in some congregations have formed their own tefilah, or prayer, groups. The pride and joy these women take in leading their services cannot help but translate into pride and joy instilled in their daughters, and from their daughters to future generations.

That pride shows itself also in the new rituals women have created to celebrate themselves and their womanhood. Birth and baby-naming ceremonies for girls, rarities just twenty years ago, are now almost standard procedure in all branches of Judaism. Bat Mitzvah services, in varying forms, are also commonplace in all the denominations. For a young Jewish woman, this passage is a form of affirming oneself, of being counted in the community of Israel.

And everywhere, women are seeking a new spirituality, a search for their own voices in texts and prayers that for so long reflected only male thinking and attitudes.[30] I have argued many times that women have to be careful not to so emphasize spirituality that they neglect intellect and study.[31] But when based on knowledge, women's spirituality, their quest for connectedness to God, their creation of ritual that speaks to their own longings and needs, is a positive force in Judaism. When women participate fully in ritual and prayer, they strengthen their own commitment and that of their family.

The world has changed drastically since the days when my great-grandmother grew all the food for her extended family even while she cared for her five grandsons, and when my grandmother cooked and cleaned for the boarders in their home and helped her husband trade with the local merchants. Neither woman would recognize any affinity to the world I inhabit and certainly not to that of my daughter. Yet the connections exist, in the strength of those women, in their devotion to their homes, and mostly in their ability to juggle many roles as they helped sustain their families and hold them together. Connections also exist in the need Jewish families had then and continue to have for support from the Jewish community. Rather than blame the women's movement and the roles it ushered in for the problems that have arisen, the community needs to understand and celebrate the many positive achievements of women in the past twenty years. Rather than see the family as doomed, or in crisis, we need to respond to the challenges change has brought. I believe that creative responses that recognize and aid the working mother, the divorced woman, the single parent can lead to a new flowering of the Jewish family and Jewish community life.

REFERENCES

1. For a discussion of the Jewish working mother, see Paula Hyman, "The Jewish Family: Looking for a Usable Past," in *On Being a Jewish Feminist*, ed. Susannah Heschel (New York: Schocken Books, 1983), pp. 19–26.

2. A good analysis of this change and its effects on women appears in Charlotte Baum, Paula Hyman, and Sonya Michel, *The Jewish Woman in America* (New York: Dial Press, 1975), pp. 227–233.

3. Philip Roth in *Portnoy's Complaint* created the most searing image of the stereotypical Jewish mother; Herman Wouk's *Marjorie Morningstar* fueled the image of the so-called "Jewish American Princess."

4. See *Memoirs of Glueckel of Hameln*, trans. Marvin Lowenthal (New York: Harper & Brothers, 1932).

5. Proverbs 31:10–31.

6. For a discussion of the denial of feminism, see Susan Faludi, *Backlash* (New York: Crown Publishers, 1991).

7. For more about the myth of the extended family, see Ferdinand Mount, *The Subversive Family: An Alternative History of Love and Marriage* (New York: Free Press, 1992).

8. 8. Calvin Goldscheider and Francis K. Goldscheider, "The Transition

to Jewish Adulthood: Education, Marriage, and Fertility" (Paper delivered at the Tenth World Congress of Jewish Studies, Jerusalem, August 1989).

9. Sylvia Barack Fishman discusses this attitude in *A Breath of Life: Feminism in the American Jewish Community* (New York: Free Press, 1993), p. 49.

10. *Highlights of the CJF 1990 National Jewish Population Survey* (New York: Council of Jewish Federations, 1991).

11. Fishman, *Breath of Life,* p. 49.

12. Susan Chira, "New Realities Fight Old Images of Mother," *New York Times,* October 4, 1992.

13. Steven M. Cohen, *Alternative Families in the Jewish Community* (New York: American Jewish Committee, 1989), p. 10.

14. Sylvia Barack Fishman, *Jewish Households, Jewish Homes: Serving American Jews in the 1990s* (Cohen Center for Modern Jewish Studies, Brandeis University, 1990), p. 13.

15. Arlie Hochschild, *The Second Shift* (New York: Viking, 1989).

16. A writer and mother of two young children, Nessa Rapoport writes, ". . . the most egalitarian husband doesn't undergo in a year the anguish we feminist Jewish mothers undergo in one day as we try to fulfill our hearts, brains and souls, each at the expense of the other." Nessa Rapoport, "A Dream of Community," *Hadassah Magazine,* January 1993, p. 18.

17. Gerson D. Cohen, from an address delivered at the 1979 Jewish Educators Assembly convention.

18. The importance of institutional attention to child care is emphasized in Ruth Pinkenson Feldman, *Child Care in Jewish Family Policy* (New York: American Jewish Committee, 1989).

19. See Frank F. Furstenberg, Jr., and Graham B. Spanier, *Recycling the Family: Remarriage After Divorce* (Newbury Park, Calif.: Sage Publications, 1987), p. 39.

20. Tamar Lewin, "Rise in Single Parenthood Is Reshaping U.S.," *New York Times,* October 5, 1992.

21. Sylvia Barack Fishman, "The Impact of Feminism on American Jewish Life," in *American Jewish Yearbook, 1989* (New York: American Jewish Committee, 1989), p. 18.

22. A number of organizations in the United States and Israel devote themselves to the problem of the agunah, among them G.E.T. (Get Equal Treatment) and Agunah, both run by Orthodox Jewish women.

23. Judith Wallerstein and Sandra Blakeslee, *Men, Women, and Children a Decade After Divorce* (New York: Ticknor & Fields, 1989).

24. Cohen, "Alternative Families," p. 10.

25. Fishman, *Jewish Households,* p. 22.

26. Ibid., p. 23.

27. For an excellent description of the position of abused wives, see Mimi Scarf, "Marriages Made in Heaven? Battered Jewish Wives," in *On Being a Jewish Feminist*, ed. Susannah Heschel (New York: Schocken Books, 1983), pp. 51–64.

28. Institutes devoted to teaching women include Drisha in New York, and Matan, Machon Lindenbaum, and Nishmat in Israel.

29. A father is obligated to circumcise his son, redeem him, teach him Torah, take a wife for him, and teach him a trade, according to the Talmud (Kiddushin 29a).

30. For some new rituals women have created, see *Lilith*, Fall 1988 and Summer 1990. On women's spirituality, see Judith Plaskow, *Standing Again at Sinai: Judaism from a Feminist Perspective* (New York: Harper Collins, 1990).

31. See Francine Klagsbrun, in *Moment* 17, no. 4 (August 1992): 14, 17.

JEWISH IDENTITY, ASSIMILATION AND INTERMARRIAGE

Irving N. Levitz

Concern that the contemporary Jewish family has lost its uniquely Jewish character and is becoming increasingly inept at either transmitting any sense of Jewish identity to its progeny or regenerating itself has been poignantly underscored by the 1990 National Jewish Population Survey (Kosmin 1991). The survey's conclusions reflect the striking degree to which American Jews are assimilating, disaffiliating, intermarrying, and disappearing.

In addition to a chronically low fertility rate which does not even minimally reach replacement levels, over half of the born Jews surveyed (52 percent) chose to marry gentile mates who remained unconverted. Currently, twice as many mixed marriages are created (Jew/Gentile) than Jewish ones, and 90 percent of the children of these intermarriages, in turn, marry non-Jews. The evident concern is that if these trends in intermarriage, low birth rate, and assimilation continue unabated, it might, indeed, spell the demise of the American Jewish community as we know it.

In a sense, there is nothing new about this concern for Jewish survival. According to some scholars, the fear of disappearing may itself be a characteristic of the Jews as a people. "There is no nation more dying than Israel," Rawidowicz asserts (Alexander 1993). The Jewish people are a "phenomenon which has almost no parallel in mankind's story: a nation that has been disappearing constantly for the last two thousand years . . . and yet still exists."

Although, from a broad historical perspective, survival anxiety notwithstanding, the Jewish people have, in fact, not disappeared as a result of assimilation, myriad individual Jews and entire Jewish communities have. The question of Jewish survival, repeatedly framed in sociological, demographic, and statistical terms, often has its most salient impact on the personal level. For the individual Jew, concern for the survival of American Jewry is most viscerally felt from a personal perspective. From this personal vantage point, concern for the demographic survival of the Jewish community is overshadowed by anxiety over the threat to the Jewish survival of one's own progeny.

Current studies and surveys do yield valuable sociological information about intermarriage trends and rates of assimilation among several groups, but reflect only obliquely on the psychological process of assimilation itself.

Who, for example, is most vulnerable to the forces of assimilation? And why? Are there factors within the modern Jewish family itself that inadvertently foster intermarriage and encourage offspring to assimilate? How strong an inoculating factor is the formation of a strong Jewish identity with regard to assimilation and intermarriage? What, from a psychological perspective, is Jewish identity?

This paper will seek to examine the phenomena of intermarriage and assimilation from the perspective of Jewish identity. It will explore, from a psychological perspective, those issues that affect the Jewish identity of individuals and families, as well as those values that inform individual life choices and life styles that either inoculate against or create vulnerability to intermarriage, assimilation, and a threatened Jewish survival.

To do this, we must first conceptualize what we mean by *Jewish identity* as a psychological construct, and then understand its relationship to an individual's likelihood of intermarrying or assimilating.

THE JEWISH IDENTITY CONSTRUCT

The role of a strong Jewish identity has long been considered to be the most potent counterforce against intermarriage, assimilation, and disaffiliation. "Jewish identity," writes Herman (1989), "relates to the conditions for the very survival of the Jewish people as a distinct entity."

Yet, there exists a cacophony of semantic confusion surrounding the concept of "Jewish identity" itself. Poorly operationalized, differentially measured, and commonly interchanged with the notion of *Jewish identification*, Jewish identity has become a murky, conceptually ambiguous construct.

In an attempt to address the problem of the inconsistent and conceptually muddled use of the term Jewish identity, Kleinman (1993) noted that "without a shared meaning for discussion, without guidelines to understand the language we use, any effort to discuss continuity and outreach is of little practical value to our professional practice". The "sociology of identity," he concluded, "has been studied much more than the inner meaning and values that are at the heart of Jewish identity" itself.

Kleinman's concerns about conceptual ambiguity are poignantly illustrated in Kosmin's (1992) discussion of current assumptions about Jewish identity. "In an individualistic, free society," he asserts, "where ethnicity and religion are voluntary, [and] the authority of tradition, family, kinship and community has decreasing force and validity, anybody is Jewish if he/she wants to be, and usually on individualistic terms. In practice, everyone is a Jew by choice."

London and Chazan (1990), in summarizing the Jewish identity literature and attempting themselves to define its parameters, essentially conceived of Jewish identity more in terms of manifest performance of public communal rituals than from a psychological, internal, value-based perspective. The study of Jewish identity "remains at the most surface level of understanding," Kleinman (1993) laments, and has been conceptualized primarily from a perspective that leaves the impression that its components are void of inner meaning, or uniquely Jewish values. Academic studies for the most part have tended to focus more on individual's *identification with* the Jewish people, rather than on their *identity as* Jews per se. The psychological differences, however, between Jewish identity and Jewish identification are significant, as are their implications for Jewish survival.

It is, therefore, important to more clearly define the construct "Jewish identity," understand how it is formed and sustained in the face of eroding forces, and how it might ultimately serve as a bulwark against intermarriage, the dissolution of Jewish family values, and total assimilation.

Identity Formation: Beliefs and Behaviors

The formation of any personal identity, i.e. an individual's sense of who he is, generally begins early in life with the internalizing of values and meanings observed in the behavior of valued role models. Identity is developed at first through a succession of identifications. It begins as modeling, or naive merging of one's self with valued others, and the mimicking of their personal characteristics. Eventually, these identifications become crystallized in the formation of internalized *schema*.

Ultimately, the schema form an identity from a combination of internalized knowledge, values, beliefs, and identifications. It is the unique set of schema that form the distinctive characteristics of each individual that become the focal source of one's personal identity.

An individual's identity, however, is not only determined by the internalized knowledge, values, and identifications that form his schema and become integral to his selfhood, but by external actions as well. Psychologically, there is a cyclical relationship between internal schema and external behavior with regard to identity (Wheelis 1973). Value schema that form identity, inform each individual's behavior. Behaviors, in turn, reflect those values, and reinforce them. As a transactional dynamic the reciprocal relationship of value informed behaviors and behaviorally reinforced values, constitute the essence of identity.

If each day with regularity, I practice my violin, then rehearse and perform in a symphony orchestra, by virtue of the constancy and repetitiveness of my behavior, I form an internalized image of myself, (i.e., an identity) as a violinist. This in turn generates further practice and musical performance.

The cyclical nature of this process of identity formation and maintenance is such, that just as internal schema drive and direct manifest behaviors, manifest behaviors, in turn, deepen and strengthen internal schema. Thus, the cyclical relationship between external action and internal schema, each affecting the other, come together into what we call *identity.*

"We are what we do" said Wheelis (1973). "Identity is the integration of behavior. . . . Action which defines a man, and describes his character, is action which has been repeated over and over and so has come in time to be a coherent and relatively independent mode of behavior."

The longer and more consistently a person acts in a specific way the more integral the behavior becomes to his identity. Whereas at first driving an automobile is a skill requiring focused attention to the technical and mechanical tasks needed to control the vehicle, by regularly and repetitively driving, less effort is soon required, and less anxious focus on technical detail. In time, some of the small component aspects of driving become integrated into the whole driving experience. I soon not only know how to drive a car, I *become a driver.* Being a driver, in turn, becomes a central force itself. Visiting distant relatives, touring other states by automobile and moving to the suburbs become possibilities only because of my new identity.

Identity, then, is not only an outcome of internalized values, skills and knowledge, but additionally has widespread and pervasive implications that affect the very construction of reality itself.

IDENTIFICATION AND IDENTITY

Despite its frequent interchangability in the literature, *identification* is not the same as *identity*. Whereas identity evolves by way of internalizing and integrating stable values consistent with one's actions, identification is generally more superficial. Identification involves taking on the admired attributes of another individual or idealized group whose characteristics are especially admired.

An ardent Yankee baseball fan, for example, may be strongly identified with the achievements of the team. He may own season tickets, never miss a home game, know every player's batting average, wear the team cap, and even sport a Yankee logo on the bumper of his car. When the Yankees win a game, his identification with the team is such that he can readily exclaim, "we won!" Everyone would agree, however, that despite his support for, and dedication to, the team, his identity is still not that of a Yankee ball player, but rather that of a fan who is strongly identified with the achievements of the team.

Though team members might also say "we won," by virtue of the fact that they actually play ball for the team, manifest the actions, attitudes, knowledge, skills, responsibilities, and values of Yankees, gives them an *identity* that differs strikingly from that of their fans. As a consequence of these kinds of internalized values, skills, sense of team purpose, and repetitive behaviors, a Yankee *identity* is formed. Yankee ball players, unlike their fans, are not merely identified with the team, they are the team.

Identity, then, unlike identification, involves a complex integration of specific values, attitudes, knowledge content, skills, and beliefs that inform specific behaviors. As these behaviors, in turn, reinforce the values and beliefs upon which they are based, the stability and continuity of identity is assured.

Identity and identification are similar, however, in at least one respect. They manifest themselves along a continuum of intensity. Just as identification can range from impassioned to peripheral, so too can the specific internalized values and external actions that constitute identity, range from extensive and all-pervasive to minimal and circumscribed. An individual, for example, who has either internalized few Jewish values, or who manifests few Jewish behaviors, will evidently not have as strong a Jewish identity as one for whom Jewish values are central in informing his/her every behavior.

Jewish Identity/Identification

What is true of identity in general, applies as well to the difference between Jewish identity and identification. *Jewish identity* consists of a complex internalized integration of specific *Jewish* schema. Rooted in Jewish values, Jewish knowledge, and uniquely Jewish beliefs, a Jewish identity informs, elicits and inspires specific Jewish behaviors.

Jewish identification on the other hand, does not require the outer manifestation of distinctively Jewish behaviors rooted in unique Jewish values. It needs only to be reflected in the degree to which an individual empathizes with, or comes to see himself as part of the destiny of the Jewish people. Identification with the destiny of the Jewish people can manifest itself, with varying degrees of intensity, in myriad ways.

Jewish identification, however, requires no overt,uniquely Jewish action. The old adage about being a good Jew at heart, which prompted the cynical designation "cardiac Jew," is an example of Jewish identification void of inner Jewish value content and uniquely Jewish behaviors. It may seem paradoxical, but clearly one can be an identified Jew, without having a Jewish identity.

This does not mean to imply that Jewish identification itself cannot be a powerful and even central component of one's sense of self. An avid Jewish identification is often associated with generous philanthropic support for Jewish causes, a sense of personal and even emotional connection to Israel, Zionism, Jewish culture, cuisine, music, art, language, history, etc. It also tends to manifest itself in preferred social contacts with other Jews, and synagogue/community center affiliation.

One, however, does not require a Jewish identity in order to be an identified Jew. In fact, one need not even be Jewish. There are many Christians who identify strongly with, and support Jewish political and philanthropic causes, especially with regard to Israel, holocaust projects, and political agendas, but can hardly be said to have a Jewish identity.

The values that inform the actions of Jewish identification, though associated with things Jewish, need not necessarily be uniquely Jewish themselves. They might be secularly based humanistic, personal or social values. A secular Jew, for example, may be identified with, and supportive of Jewish institutions and causes for humanitarian reasons rather than for the fulfillment of a divine imperative to give tzedekah (charity). Because his identity is essentially secular and not intrinsically rooted in a Jewish value base, humanistic values would most likely inform his charitable behavior rather than a religious imperative. In this instance, it doesn't matter much from a practical perspective, nor does it diminish from the goodness of the act. It is only that the act itself emanates from a secular rather than from a religious value base, and is therefore a manifestation of Jewish identification rather than an expression of Jewish identity.

Similarly, a secular Israeli Jew, who speaks Hebrew, serves in the Israeli army, and is even knowledgeable about Judaic beliefs and Jewish history may still not have any semblance of a Jewish identity, but rather an identity as an Israeli. As Herman's (1989) studies indicated, a significant number of Israelis do not, in fact, have Jewish identities per se, as there are those who lack even an identification with things Jewish. This, despite their Israeli citizenship and social integration in a Jewish state.

Analogously, what is true for team identity in baseball applies as well to Jewish identity/identification. There are players and there are fans. Each fulfills a specific role. Both contribute to the team, but each in a different way.

Jewish Identity: Critical Values

The essential feature of Jewish identity is its internalization of distinctively Jewish values, knowledge, and beliefs, which manifest themselves in characteristic Jewish behaviors. Identity more than identification appears to be the most potent antidote to intermarriage and assimilation.

"While most American Jews identify themselves as such and are prepared to stand up and be counted as Jews," Herman (1989), notes, "many of those identifying as Jews are nevertheless swept away by the tide of assimilation, unless they develop a cultural distinctiveness of Jewish identity which sets them apart as different." Jewish identification alone may simply be insufficient to thwart the tide of assimilation and intermarriage.

According to Herman (1989), the core system of values that distinctively delineates Jewish identity from identification is rooted in Jewish religious tradition, rather than in the peripheral ethnic characteristics or cultural reflections of that tradition. He notes that "a secular Jewishness without roots in Jewish tradition often lacks the strength to withstand the forces of assimilation in the non-Jewish majority culture".

It is not surprising, then, that in all of his studies of Jewish identity, Herman found that "religious observance is the crucial variable in a Jewish identity. Religiously observant respondents stand highest on the ladder of Jewish identity, followed by those in the traditionalist category, and lowest on the ladder are the non-religious."

It is difficult, indeed, if not erroneous, to speak of uniquely Jewish values without in some way anchoring them within a normative religious framework. Since the dawning of Jewish history, the core essence of Jewish identity and the antidote to assimila-

tion has always consisted of normative religious values, knowledge, beliefs, and distinctive religiously based behaviors.

Religious/Secular Values

Jewish identity in the modern world, however, is such that one
could not consider its development and maintenance without
taking into account the modifying influences of secular values on
that identity.

In reality, Jews living in the modern world, even those with
strong, uniquely Jewish identities, do in fact internalize secular
values which tend to interface with, influence, modify, and even
conflict with their Jewish values. It is rare to find Jews who are
unaffected by the values, beliefs, and normative behaviors of
modern secular society. Even amongst the world's most seques-
tered Jews, who vehemently reject modern secular influences, and
who have the most intense Jewish identities- the *haredim* of
Jerusalem, traces of modern influences can be found (Heilman
1992).

The personal identity of the contemporary Jew, understood as a
function of its many elemental component parts and their degree
of integration, is comprised of both secular and Jewish values.
The differences among Jews, and their vulnerability to intermarriage and assimilation, may indeed lie in the *ratio* of internalized
secular to Jewish values. In order to understand the differing
motives, attitudes, and actions of Jews who intermarry, in contrast to those who do not, it is important to understand the
nature of this ratio of internalized secular and religious values.
Evidently if the ratio is strongly weighted in favor of Jewish values the likelihood of assimilation and subsequent intermarriage is
significantly less than where there is a strong secular to Jewish
ratio.

What ratio of Jewish/secular identity, however, is sufficient to
prevent an individual from considering intermarriage? Is there a
critical point of vulnerability? In the constellation of Jewish and

secular values, are specific Jewish values more inoculating than others? What are the critical Jewish and secular values that either inoculate against, or promote intermarriage and assimilation?

Modern Secularism: Religious Values and Intermarriage

Prager (1988) could not have stated it more emphatically when he wrote that "it is not Christianity that challenges our childrens' Jewish identity. It is secularism". "An open secular society", he warns, "with all its advantages, poses a far greater challenge than does a Christian America.... while the modern secular world is considerably *less* dangerous to Jewish bodies, it is considerably more dangerous to Jewish survival."

What is it that concerns Jewish thinkers about modern secularism? What is it that seems to be so antithetical to normative Judaism and threatening to Jewish survival?

Whatever else it might be, modern secularism is a humanly constructed, rationally based, principled belief system, which, not unlike religion, includes normative assumptions, expectations and ideals, that provide the standard and context of acceptable human behavior.

Though historically, secularism from its origin as a late seventeenth-century European ideology strongly challenged a God-centered perspective, today it appears significantly less antagonistic toward a religious worldview. It is not so much that for modern secularists religion is no longer antithetical. It is simply that religion is irrelevant. It is only on those occasions when religious postures impede secular objectives, threaten to interfere with secular lifestyle, or attempt to define the Jewishness of secular co-religionists, that religion is confronted antagonistically. It is otherwise of little import.

Modern secularism differs from normative Judaism in several significant ways. To the secular mind "man is the measure of all things". The centrality of man, with all of its ramifications, is one of the most·prominent features in the ideology of modernism.

Influenced by the humanistic notion of *individualism*, modern society places significant emphasis on man's intrinsic right to choose freely in all areas of belief, personal values, and standard of behavior. Man himself is the sole arbiter of his personal philosophy, worldview, lifestyle, personal goals, and aspirations. Man himself determines how he wishes to live, with whom he wishes to live, whether he wishes to cohabit, marry, or have children, and certainly how he wishes to raise them. So long as his behavior does not impede the freedom and rights of others, he is free to exercise personal choice.

Individualism is supported by other tenets of secular philosophy that affect assimilation and intermarriage, namely *pluralism*, and *universalism*. These ideologies embrace the premise that each person has the intrinsic right to freely choose his/her own standards and beliefs. Since all people are created equal, every belief has equal validity, as every value is equally good. When these pluralistic values are internalized and integrated into one's identity, their impact on one's choice to marry out of faith is both significant and self evident. When behaviors are informed by individualism and pluralism, marrying out of faith is not only a matter of an individual's prerogative and personal preference, it is also an essential component of the American ethos and the fulfillment of a sacralized American ideal (Spickard 1989).

These premises are in stark contradistinction to traditional Jewish ideology. From the traditional Jewish perspective, God, not man, has primacy in determining the standards of acceptable behavior. The task of man is not to act primarily on the basis of his own will, but rather to wilfully submit his will to a Divine imperative.

For the Jew whose identity is formed by traditional religious values, the only valid use of personal volition is in the paradoxical choice to restrict that volition and choose to submit to both divine and rabbinic authority. Personal preferences, predilections and passions are subdued in order to be in concert with that

Divine imperative - as reflected in halacha. Individual growth and development is measured by how successfully the will is conquered and the submissive posture attained. "He surrenders authority over his existence in the realization that he cannot be his own authority" (Soloveitchick 1965) . For a Jew whose identity has integrated these principles, intermarriage, which is prohibited by biblical decree, is so ego alien as to make it an unthinkable option.

> and you should not marry them,—your daughter should not be given to his son, and his daughter should not be taken for your son; for they will turn your son from following Me, and serve other gods . . . and you will be quickly destroyed.
>
> (Deut.7:3–4)

Submission of personal will to that of a Divine authority (or any authority for that matter) is a notion that is particularly antithetical to the humanistic ideals of individualism and personal freedom. Primacy of self is not easily reconciled with an ideology requiring submission to a higher authority, with its consequential inhibition of will, behavioral conformity, prescribed traditional norms, and constraints on personal freedom.

Secular Family Values

For the modern secular Jewish family, society's secular ideology absorbed as family values, form the identities of its members, and sensitize them for intermarriage. Intermarriage, in that sense, is a process more akin to a journey than to an event, and is the result rather than the cause of assimilation. "If intermarriage can be viewed as the outgrowth of leaving the fold rather than as the essence of it, then one can better focus on the need to inform parents of their crucial role in the transmission of Jewish behavior and values" (Eichorn 1974).

As a practicing family psychologist, I am engaged with increasing frequency, in a cataclysmic, yet common, drama of secular, Jewishly identified families, agonizing over the impending intermarriage of an adult child. Adult children, on the other hand, often express bewilderment and confusion at what appears to them a sudden parental surge of Jewish consciousness just at a time when they have fallen in love.

It is difficult and often futile for secularized Jewish parents, even for those with strong Jewish identifications, to dissuade their adult children from an out of faith marriage. At the point when grown children have already been socialized to secular values, formed identities based on the ideals of individual rights, personal freedom of choice, and cultural pluralism, the plea from parents for Jewish continuity rings hollow. Once a strong secular identity has been formed, too many values inform the decision to marry out of faith. The very secular ideal that promulgates complete integration into mainstream American society, also in essence fosters intermarriage. For, as noted earlier, within the context of an American ethos, intermarriage itself is an ideal (Spickard 1989).

In addition to absorbing and promulgating modern society's values of individualism and pluralism, it is not uncommon for the secularized Jewish family to view its Jewishness from a universalistic perspective as well. Where this is true, the principles of universalism erode any sense of Jewish distinctiveness, or uniquely Jewish purpose and destiny. Jewish beliefs, behaviors and values that are distinctively Jewish are perceived as narrow, particularistic, and ethnocentric. They are easily rejected for more open minded, uncritical, positive regard for all ethnic and religious groups. "What difference does it make who a person is or what his beliefs are," pleaded a young Jewish woman with her parents in a recent family therapy session, "as long as he is a good person." She was referring to her gentile fiance, and from a secular perspective, her argument was sound. The very principles of pluralism and universalism, with which she was nurtured and which formed her identity, in effect negated there being anything special about being Jewish, remaining Jewish, or marrying Jewish.

Growing up in a secular Jewish family, one's perspective about tradition and the Jewish past is that it is associated, at best, with the quaint and the colorful. At worst it evokes images of the archaic and the primitive. This is hardly an incentive to strive for its continuity.

By essentially championing the values of individualism and primacy of self over submission to a divine norm, personal freedom over religious imperatives, universalism and pluralism over cultural and religious distinctiveness, and change over tradition, the secular Jewish family nurtures an essentially non Jewish identity, inadvertently laying the groundwork for disaffiliation, assimilation, and intermarriage.

Traditional Jewish Perspectives

Individuals growing up in traditional Jewish families, on the other hand, embrace a value system that differs sharply from that of their secular coreligionists. One's beliefs, as to whether this universe is God-centered or man-centered, has profound ramifications, not only for how reality per se is structured, but how intermarriage itself is perceived.

Since, in the realm of Jewish ideology, God's will is primary, the rule of God's Law (Torah) determines the standards and parameters of appropriate behavior. It is within this framework that intermarriage is seen as unequivocally prohibited. Marrying a Gentile has for thousands of years been equated with death itself,as those who intermarried were seen as severing the chain of Jewish continuity. Intermarriage, as spiritual death, was mourned by parents much the same way they would a child's physical demise.

This perception of intermarriage as spiritual death, and the severing of the generational chain, has for centuries served as a significant constraint on intermarriage among traditional Jews. In addition, however, other value factors have impacted as well.

Tradition by its very nature is embedded in a past that is associated with greater authenticity and truth than the present. For centuries, the Jew not only valued the past but yearned for it, attempted to understand it in order to emulate it, and transcend the present as a way of experiencing a glimmer of it. The present was only meaningful as a link between past and future, for the past contained within it the revelation at Sinai, the time of great prophets, divinely inspired sages, and the richness of an authentic Jewish life in the land of Israel.

A major objective of marriage from the traditional Jewish perspective is to preserve that past. A couple is expected to bond together in love, for the express purpose of building a dynamic context for transmitting the values of the Jewish past to the generations of a Jewish future. By creating a *Bayis ne-emon b'yisrael,* a home committed to the authentic traditions of this Jewish past, replete with uniquely Jewish acts, symbols, rituals, beliefs and behaviors, a couple aspires to assure Jewish continuity by giving their children distinctively Jewish identities. With this as the raison d'etre for family life, marrying out of faith is not merely alien, it is considered a catastrophic betrayal, and a severing of the chain of generations. For most of the intermarrying secular Jews whom I see professionally, however, severing the chain of Jewish continuity is a concern of little consequence.

THE TRADITIONAL COMMUNITY CONTEXT

The context of a traditional Jewish community, with its distinctive Jewish ethos appears to be a critical variable with regard to Jewish identity, not only as a dynamic vehicle for Jewish identity formation, but also as a structure for its maintenance. It is within this context that the clear boundaries of acceptable and deviant norms are clearly prescribed. It is here that expectations for personal deportment, social demeanor, appropriate dress, and distinctive lifestyle are made manifest. Jewish identity is reinforced daily by the adoption of Jewish names, the wearing of identifying

Jewish garb, and recurrent ritual behaviors.

In addition to the social and community factors that reinforce a dominant Jewish identity and offer a dynamic arena for its expression, specific behaviors performed regularly augment and strengthen that identity. Not only does daily prayer provide a regular opportunity for religious connectedness, but the social context of synagogue life further strengthens the individual's religious identity by giving him a sense of belonging to a community that both values and promulgates distinctively Jewish values. It is this sense of being an integral part of the Jewish community that further enhances and reinforces one's sense of Jewish identity.

The behavior that appears to be particularly effective in strengthening the individual's sense of Jewish identity, however, is that of Torah study itself. Torah study, on a serious level, is more than just an intellectual or cognitive exercise alone. Experientially, one enters a world whose premises differ significantly from the secular world. The world of Torah study is premised on faith, buttressed by profound reasoning, and charged with the divine imperative to engage in it day and night. For the traditional Jew the study of Torah is not only central to his way of life, but defines his purpose for living and his role in the Jewish scheme of things. It is his responsibility not only to learn Torah but to perpetuate it and transmit it to the next generation.

For those traditional Jewish families who experience a sense of commitment to religious ideals, derive meaning from its rituals, beliefs and behavioral norms, and sufficient satisfactions from its lifestyle, their progeny appear protected from assimilation and intermarriage. When these traditional values are either deficient, ineffectually transmitted, or subjected to distortion due to family dysfunction, then even a traditional family will be vulnerable to disaffiliation, secularization and assimilation.

Despite the fact that a cultural chasm is created between those who live within the traditional world and that of society at large, it is this very distancing and conscious separation from secular values that provides the safeguards perceived to be essential for maintaining a predominantly Jewish identity with its passionate commitment to the perpetuation of Jewish peoplehood and tradition.

Although there is little doubt that traditionalists live *in* the modern world, it is evident that they are not *of* it. Nor is it considered their *real* world. For the secularist, the real world is the material, empirical world in which he currently resides. It is the here and now world, richly endowed with a multi-colored life tapestry. It is a world to be enjoyed, conquered, mastered and modified.

Secular philosophies assert that the sensory world is essentially all there is, and basically all one has. Psychologically, philosophically, culturally, ecologically and experientially investing oneself in this world is indeed a secular ideal. The implicit impact of this value on intermarriage is such that if one finds pleasure, love, companionship, and common interest with another individual, in the here and now, survival of the religion into which one is born is inconsequential. An emotional bond with a 3,500-year-old people is both too mystical for the modern palate, and irrelevant to the here and now.

Finally, the primary value in secular Jewish families placed on achievement of personal, financial, and social success, often inform the choice of sending children to a prestigious out of town college. It is within that milieu that the formation of a secularized, Jewishly indifferent, identity is completed.

Campus Ideology: The College Experience

What the secular Jewish family fosters in the identity development of its children, comes to full maturity on the college campus. American Jewish families have shown a proclivity to embrace high culture, promote high socio-economic aspirations, and encourage higher education. Thus, "Jews are three times as likely to be products of Western liberal higher education with its

emphasis on open mindedness, individuality and personal fulfillment than are average Americans," writes Kosmin (1992). The
college experience may not only be the most pervasive form of
exposure to secular values, it may also have the most consequential impact with regard to Jewish survival. Not only does its ideology lay the social value base for intermarriage, but its precincts
provide a ready laboratory for interreligious dating and intermarriage.

University environments are meant to teach the prevailing
ethic, and the more educationally impactful the institution, the
more likely are its students to internalize its values, be shaped by
its mores, and socialized by its norms.

Given the secular norms of university life, students are covertly
or overtly encouraged to integrate and interdate, or risk being
perceived of as intolerant, insular, or provincial. In some college
settings it is simply seen as deviant, biased, and a violation of the
prevailing liberal norm.

Within the context of academia, with all of its sanctioning and
promulgation of secular norms, a superficial Jewish identification
is hardly sufficient to withstand the secular influences of college
life, and stem the tide of assimilation.

By the time a family seeks treatment for the stress caused by an
impending intermarriage, the die is already cast. The values,
inadvertently promulgated by the family itself, and reinforced on
the college campus, that prescribe intermarriage have long been
internalized, and a romantic relationship has already been
allowed to develop. Being a Jew at this point is no longer as
important as being in love.

Primacy of the Romantic Ideal

The primacy and idealization of love and romance in contemporary society is another factor that plays a critical role in the
increase of intermarriage. Being in love has no rival in the hierar-
chy of values that determine the direction of a relationship.

Within the framework of the romantic ideal, issues that arise out of differing religious, cultural, or ethnic backgrounds, are seen only as exciting challenges to be overcome rather than impediments. The conviction that "love conquers all" leaves a couple believing that love is sufficient to overcome whatever differences exist between them so long as their strong romantic feelings continue.

It is not that romance does not play a role in the sphere of religious values. It is that love within a traditional Jewish context simply does not supersede the value of Jewish continuity.

Love itself is also a manifestation of identity. Tevye, the central character in *Fiddler on the Roof*, when confronted by the impending marriage of his daughter to a gentile, laments that,

"A bird and a fish could fall in love, but where will they build a nest?" Tevye's anguish is palpable, but his metaphor is flawed. Where intermarriage is concerned, birds do not marry fish, they marry other birds. Intermarriage is rarely anything but birds of a feather building nests together. Intimacy, friendship, and social bonding are generally premised on shared values (Bennis et al. 1973). An individual with a strong Jewish identity therefore, is most unlikely to choose a mate with a modern secular identity. Conversely, it is shared societal values that make secular Jew and secular Gentile so seemingly compatible. Since the divorce rate among intermarried couples is several times the norm (Bayme 1990), this compatibility is often more illusory than real.

Given a relationship, therefore, where there are shared secular values, compatible differences, physical attraction, and a supportive societal norm, love followed by commitment is all too often an inevitability. This combination of factors, indeed, may form the context for the majority of Jewish/Gentile marriages today. With whom one falls in love, contrary to the notion that it is a cupid like phenomenon, is therefore also a function of identity and internalized values, as well.

Summary

This paper attempts a reconceptualization of Jewish identity based on psychological principles of identity formation. Identity formation is not, however, a static phenomenon, but rather an ongoing dynamic process. If that were not so, change would never be possible.

The impact of secular values on the identity of modern Western Jews is pervasive and formidable. The major premise of this paper is that essentially, these values are the harbinger of a disappearing American Jewry. Unlike traditional Jewish values, they promote and advance beliefs and behaviors that not only encourage intermarriage but sees it as a higher good. In the absence of internalized Jewish values, sophisticated Jewish knowledge that emanates from serious Torah study, informed and repetitive practice of uniquely Jewish behaviors, and a distinctively Jewish communal context, the formation of strong Jewish identities is unlikely to occur among the majority of American Jews. Unless these factors are increased, and it is unlikely that they will be, Jewish identification is also likely to diminish. There are indications that this is already occurring.

The consequences are indeed grave, and it is difficult to be optimistic with regard to the majority of American Jews in light of current surveys and clinical data. Some American Jews, specifically those with strong internalized Jewish identities, will indeed survive across the generations. Those with Jewish identification alone, unless buttressed by a distinctive Jewish identity, have a significantly lower probability of survival. For the majority of assimilated American Jews, Jewish survival itself may very soon be of little personal concern. They, like many before them, may simply vanish as Jews.

REFERENCES

Alexander, E. 1993. The ever-dying people. *The Bridge.* PNAI, Summer.

Bayme, S. 1990. Changing perceptions of intermarriage. *Journal of Jewish Communal Service* 66:212–223

Bennis, W., Berlew, D., Schein, E., and Steele, F. 1973. *Interpersonal Dynamics: Essays and Readings on Human Interaction.* Brooks Cole.

Eichorn, D. 1974. *Jewish Intermarriages: Fact and Fiction.* Satellite Beach, Fla.: Satellite Books.

Herman, S. 1977. *Jewish Identity: A Social Psychological Perspective.* Sage Library of Social Research, vol. 48. Beverly Hills, Calif.

———. 1989. The study of contemporary Jewish identity. In *Facing The Future*, ed. S. Bayme, p. 203. New York: Ktav.

Kleinman, D. 1993. Jewish identity, continuity and outreach: Some theoretical and personal reflections. *Journal of Jewish Communal Service*, May.

Kosmin, B. 1992. The permeable boundaries of being Jewish in America. *Moment* 17, no. 4:32–51.

———, et al. 1991. *Highlights of the CJF 1990 National Jewish Population Survey.* New York: Council of Jewish Federations.

London, P., and Chazan, B.. 1990. *Psychology and Jewish Identity Education.* New York: American Jewish Committee.

Prager, D. 1988. Raising a Jewish child in a non-Jewish world. *Moment* 13, no. 8.

Spickard, P. 1989. *Mixed Blood: Intermarriage and Ethnic Identity in Twentieth Century America.* Madison: University of Wisconsin Press.

Soloveitchik, J. 1965. The lonely man of faith. *Tradition* 7, no. 2.

Wheelis, A. 1973. *How People Change.* New York: Harper & Row.

CLINICAL ISSUES IN INTERMARRIAGE: A FAMILY SYSTEMS APPROACH

Mark I. Sirkin

OVERVIEW OF THEORETICAL AND ETHICAL ISSUES

When a Jewish child is ritually welcomed into the Jewish community, it is traditional to wish three things for him or her: Torah, mitzvah, and chuppah. That is, that the child should know God, do good deeds, and have a Jewish marriage. Torah represents the knowledge of God, as well as a connection to the past, a connection to Jewish peoplehood. Mitzvah represents acting ethically in the world, a connection to the needs of the present. Chuppah, the Jewish wedding canopy, represents a Jewish marriage, a Jewish family with Jewish children, and a connection to the future. One can only appreciate the pain and panic caused by intermarriage when one envisions a world without a future. For many Jewish families facing intermarriage, it is the end of history (Packouz 1976).

For many other Jewish families facing intermarriage, however, this is just one more step on the road to assimilation and acceptance. While the marriage may not be quite as joyful as one to another Jew, neither is it a reason to mourn. So there may be a little less Yiddishkeit in the home, but hasn't that been the trend for the past century at least? Intermarriage, for these families, is one more step away from the ghetto, one less demand of Jewish law to constrain them.

These two views represent the extremes of Jewish attitudes toward religious intermarriage. Taken together they form the parameters of a debate that may be the most vital, and vociferous, controversy in modern American Jewry at the close of the twentieth century. This is a debate that will impact on Jewish policy, Jewish education, and every other aspect of Jewish life. The focus of this paper will be on the impact of intermarriage on the Jewish family. Specifically, it will examine the role of clinicians (i.e., Jewish social workers, Jewish psychologists, and Jewish agency professionals) as they struggle to serve families and individuals who come to them for help. First, however, the full scope of the problems that intermarriage presents must be appreciated.

IMPACT OF INTERMARRIAGE ON THE JEWISH FAMILY

The Data

The Council of Jewish Federations reported in its 1990 National Jewish Population Survey that over the previous five years, Jewish intermarriage rates had reached 52 percent (Kosmin et al. 1991). Although these data were not surprising to anyone who has watched intermarriage statistics climb over the past twenty years, 52 percent seemed to represent a watershed, i.e., more than half of all Jews currently marrying, marry non-Jews. But sociologists remark that it is not the increase in intermarriage that is alarming but the *rate* of increase, quintupling over the past twenty years (Fishman et al. 1990). Nor should it surprise anyone that the intermarriage rate shows no sign of leveling off and that recent estimates are now as high as 57 percent (Paul 1993).

The crucial question is not how many people are intermarrying, but what happens when a couple intermarries. More specifically, what is the impact on the individual's and couple's Jewish identity and the Jewish identity of their offspring? These data have been surprisingly consistent over time. In the late 1970s, Mayer and Sheingold (1979) concluded that "in most mixed marriages, the born-Jewish spouse affirms a Jewish identity, but does little to act on this affirmation" (p. 29). In a more recent study, Medding, Tobin, Fishman, and Rimor (1992) conclude that "in all, the data indicate that mixed marriage and the level of Jewish identification are strongly negatively related" and "that mixed marriage must be regarded as a virtual bar to the achievement of a high level of Jewish identification" (p. 37). In addition, it seems that these marriages are less stable, with approximately 50 percent ending in divorce, twice the national average for endogamous Jewish marriages (Kosmin et al. 1989). Remarriages are dramatically more likely to be to non-Jews than to Jews (Mayer 1985).

The Jewish identity of the children of intermarriage seems to fare worse than the Jewish identity of their intermarried parents (Mayer 1983). Of the children of intermarriage, only about one-third identify as Jewish, and only one in ten will marry a Jew. To illustrate some of the cause for concern about intermarriage, a simple extrapolation of these data demonstrates that for every 100 Jews who intermarry, only about 10 percent of their off-spring will marry Jews in the second generation, and by the third generation, only 1 percent of the original group will have off-spring who identify as Jewish.

There is some small room for optimism, and it lies in the data regarding conversion (Mayer and Avgar 1987). If the non-Jewish spouse converts to Judaism, then these marriages are actually higher in Jewish identity and practice than endogamous marriages. The children of these marriages are more likely to marry Jewish partners. Technically, these are no longer intermarriages but conversionary marriages.

Intermarriage, which was once relatively rare in Jewish families, is now becoming commonplace. The reactions to intermarriage, which were once uniformly negative and rejecting, can now be arrayed on a continuum. Rare nowadays is the family that sits *shiva* for an intermarried member as if he or she had died. But reactions can still be extremely negative, even tragic, for a family facing intermarriage. At the other extreme are families so tentatively connected to Judaism that they voice no objection to a prospective intermarriage. Between these extremes lies an unspecified majority of Jewish families who still find intermarriage distasteful, unpleasant, or downright unacceptable. I would like to suggest that we refer to intermarriages in such families as *"family dystonic intermarriage"* to convey that the intermarriage is objectionable to at least some part of the family system.

The Robert M. Beren Center

The Robert M. Beren Center exists to help families facing family dystonic intermarriage. Established at the Ferkauf Graduate School of Psychology at Yeshiva University, the Beren Center helps families that have members contemplating intermarriage. The goal of the Center is to provide psychological counseling to individuals and couples contemplating intermarriage and their parents, siblings, and extended family. The Center targets families for which rabbinic intervention, when sought, has been ineffective. As a matter of policy, and when clinically indicated, the Center will refer couples who have already intermarried to services that exist for them in the community.

While the policy of the Center is not to encourage intermarriage, nevertheless we believe this decision is ultimately in the hands of those contemplating the marriage. These are never simple decisions, and our goal is to assist our clients to think through all the ramifications and to explore alternatives to intermarriage. The Beren Center endeavors to remain faithful to the Orthodox Jewish principles upon which it was founded as well as to honestly help the individuals and families who seek our services.

Most parents approach us with the hope that we will help avert the intermarriage. Some approach us looking for help to accept, or make the best of, the inevitable. They may have additional concerns after the intermarriage, such as getting a clearer message across to their other children of the importance of marrying Jewishly, or how to maintain Jewish traditions for their mixed-heritage grandchildren. Young people contemplating intermarriage use our services because they want to know the facts and to be prepared for the problems. Often they will come because another part of the family system, usually their parents, are in anguish over their plans. Regardless of outcome, most families report feeling helped by our services.

The experience that these families and individuals have of "feeling helped" is the primary justification for the existence of the Robert M. Beren Center. Yet it would be disingenuous not to admit that there may be a conflict between simply "helping" and remaining dedicated to the Orthodox Jewish principles which are also important to the Center and its institutional sponsor, Yeshiva University. The conflict arises because "helping" is a relative term, usually defined by the person in need of help, while the Orthodox opposition to intermarriage is independent of individual desires.

This conflict of values is not unique to the Beren Center. Nor is it limited to problems related to intermarriage. Most clinicians and clinics function in settings which endorse some values over others. This is especially true of clinics under religious auspices, but even government clinics must be guided by certain values, i.e., the values embedded in the U.S. Constitution. In addition, many clinicians have their own values as well as professional codes of ethics, which guide them in their day-to-day work. How are these personal values balanced with institutional values on the one hand, and clients' needs on the other? Before turning to a clinical model developed to work with intermarriage, we must first address this ethical dilemma in clinical practice.

THE CLINICAL PERSPECTIVE REEXAMINED

What Is the Clinical Perspective?

Throughout history, people in pain or distress have always sought help. The helper, in his or her role as physician, healer, expert, or shaman, was able to help by dint of specialized knowledge that seemed relevant to the individual in need, the family that brought the person in need, and the society that sanctioned the healer's role. Over the past two hundred years, the clinic, and the clinical perspective, have evolved to include the aura of science, with all the implications of omnipotence and omniscience that accompany it (Foucault 1975).

The treatment of psychological problems in the clinic has always occupied a border region between the application of natural science, as in a case of appendicitis, and the application of moral values, as in family counseling. The application of natural science is the essence of the medical model, an approach to illness that looks for the underlying biological causes of disease. One classic case used to justify the medical model was that of dementia caused as a result of an earlier infection by the syphilis bacterium; in other words, a clear-cut case of a mental problem with roots in a biological infection. The medical model is built upon such classic cases, and many modern-day psychiatrists still search for the underlying biological causes of all psychological problems (cf. American Psychiatric Association 1987).

Although psychotherapy borrows some of its authorization from the medical model, we must admit that the work clinical psychologists or clinical social workers do as psychotherapists is fundamentally different from the pure application of this model. Perry London has made this case eloquently in his landmark book *The Modes and Morals of Psychotherapy* (1986):

> Insofar as they are concerned with the diagnosis and treatment of illness, modern psychotherapists have grown up in the tradition of medicine. But the nature of the ailments they deal with and the way they treat them set them apart from physicians and in some ways make them function like clergymen. . . . [Psychotherapists] are clinicians. And much of the material with which they deal, as clinicians, is neither intelligible nor usable without thought to some system of values. . . . Moral considerations may largely dictate how they define their clients' needs, how they operate in the therapeutic session, and how they sometimes define "treatment" and "cure" and even "reality."

(pp. 5–6)

A clinical approach to helping people with problems related to intermarriage necessarily involves some system of values, and the therapist should have an awareness of that system.

In Jewish agencies and clinics, the clinical perspective must differ from the rabbinic perspective. Not that there is necessarily a contradiction between the two, but at the very least, they represent different roles and different choices for both the help-seeker and the help-giver. The rabbi's role, primarily, is to help congregants interpret Jewish law and live better Jewish lives. The psychotherapist, for the most part, seeks to treat clients without recourse to the divine, with an emphasis on human resources and social supports. The latter utilizes professional knowledge with its roots in science, while the former utilizes the justice and mercy of Jewish tradition. To use a metaphor from the marketplace, the two are "vendors," and the "consumer" is free to choose the product that most suits him or her.

The treatment goals of the clinician are by definition more relativistic than the goals of the rabbi. From a rabbinic perspective, intermarriage is wrong and a rabbi-in-role must take that stand. The clinician may ask the more relativistic question "Is intermarriage good for you?", and the family therapist might add, "What will be the effects on your family?" In addition, the clinician is free, indeed encouraged, to see the presenting problem as the tip of the iceberg, in order to discern and treat underlying causes of conflict and unhappiness. It is the rare rabbi who will respond to a halachic question with the query, "Is it good for you?" or "What makes that question important to you?"

The Myth of Being Value-Free

Psychotherapists are taught in their training to be "value-free" so that they do not inadvertently impose their will or values upon their clients. There is even a term, "countertransference," that implies that the therapist has let slip the veil of professional imperturbability and may have irrational thoughts and feelings about a client. Yet as London (1986) reminded us, psychotherapy is an inherently moralistic enterprise. How can any professional steer a course in the stormy sea of a client's life without the rudder of morals and the compass of ethics?

A diagnosis often provides the initial justification to begin the work of psychotherapy. It is standard operating procedure in most clinics, especially when third-party reimbursement is sought, to provide a clinical diagnosis as justification for treatment. This diagnosis tells us, in the vernacular, what is "wrong" with the patient. Diagnoses for mental problems, other than organic disorders, are in essence value judgments about behavior and feelings masked in terms of sickness and health (Szasz 1970).

Based on the preferred school of a given psychotherapist, entire lexicons exist for the identification and treatment of problems with psychotherapy. Within each lexicon, there is a criterion by which "health," "improvement," "wholeness," "normal development," "O.K.-ness," or "functionality" is judged. Freud, for example, held the criterion to be, "Where id was, there shall ego be" (Freud 1923). Mahler, Pine, and Bergman (1975) sought the achievement of separation/individuation from the maternal object as a criterion for wholeness. The Kohutians believe in the transmutation of internalized selfobjects as the goal of psychotherapy (Kohut 1977). Eriksonian ego psychologists look for the mastery of specific life-stage tasks as a criterion for proper development (Erikson 1950). Family therapist Murray Bowen (1978) holds that the differentiation of self in the context of the family is the goal for which one should ultimately strive. I have suggested that it is the balance between autonomy and interdependence that is the criterion of successful psychotherapy and development (Sirkin and Rueveni 1992).[1]

One cannot enter into the conduct of psychotherapy without a working model of human functioning and the proper ends toward which that functioning should strive. There are some areas where professionals can fool themselves into believing that they are just helping a "sick" person to become "healthy"; cases involving major mental illness are examples. But in many situations, certainly in cases involving counseling people about intermarriage, the way is less clear. Many questions abound, with few simple answers: Should a therapist ever encourage or discourage an action? What if a course of action is good for one person in a family but not for another? What if a course of action is good for someone, or even a whole family, but bad for one's ethnic group? How should a psychotherapist react when a client's contemplated course of action is personally anathema to the therapist? How should one act when institutional values run counter to one's professional values?

Ethical Dilemmas in Working with Intermarriage

Since not all therapists who work with intermarriage are alike, different conflicts may arise for different professionals. Neither will problems dealing with intermarriage appear in isolation, but they will be part of the larger context of one's professional and personal life.

The first and most important principle I will suggest is that psychotherapists must be honest with themselves. Without this standard all attempts at intervention are suspect. How does one feel about the presenting problem, how can one best help the person in need? Can the therapist honestly assist the client in exploring all options?

The second principle is that the therapist must strive to be honest with the client. Therapists who cannot be neutral should be able to discuss their biases, as biases, with their clients. Ultimately, it is the client's decision to work with a given therapist, and the therapist, by being candid about potential biases, allows the client to make an informed decision. For example, when clients ask me, usually within the first five minutes, what my stance is about intermarriage, I admit that I find intermarriage problematical but go on to say that I believe I have something to offer them despite my bias and that, ultimately, I will respect their right to choose the course of action that they deem is best for them.

There are extra burdens for the halachic (religious) Jew, and for any psychotherapist who abides by a strict moral code. Among the many constraints on behavior that Jewish law imposes, it is also incumbent upon the halachic Jew not to assist anyone to violate the code. Again I would invoke the first and second principles mentioned above: honesty to oneself and honesty to one's client. Ultimately, our professional obligation is to act in the best interests of the client, even if that means we cannot work with a specific person or a specific problem.

For therapists working in institutional settings, there may be dilemmas in which the goals of the institution, on the one hand, and the professional, and personal, values of the therapist, on the other, collide. For example, someone opposed to intermarriage may be asked to work with intermarried couples. At first, this may seem like a conflict for which the only solution is to admit to a clash of values and withdraw from treatment. However, some of my colleagues, opposed to intermarriage, have remained to run groups of this sort while rationalizing that through their help some of these couples might return to Judaism and the non-Jewish spouse will decide to convert. While I am not qualified to comment on the halachic propriety of their decision, it is clear that they have weighed the complicated moral issues and made a decision that is faithful to their professional and institutional selves. They can readily discuss these issues with group members when and if questions arise about their personal beliefs.

The ability to be honest and open about one's moral dilemmas is a good litmus test and helps keep the clinician focused. By way of contrast, I know a clinician who runs groups for interfaith couples and their parents and is himself intermarried. His intermarriage is not something he readily discusses with groups or the Jewish agencies that hire him. When I watch him run groups, I detect a hidden agenda of helping parents and couples accept the intermarriage and move on, whether or not they are ready or willing to do this. I do not think his intermarriage precludes him from running these groups. I do believe that his inability to be honest and open, even at the risk of alienating some, hampers his capacity to do good clinical work.

The most difficult ethical dilemma, not just for the clinician, but for rabbis and parents alike, is to watch the exercise of free choice toward ends with which we disagree. For the committed Jew to watch someone intermarry, or worse, convert to another religion, is painful. But free choice is the *sine qua non* of moral behavior, and without it none of us are free; without it, the work we do as clinicians is pointless. The goal of our clinical work, therefore, is not to subvert free choice by persuasion or guile. Our goal is to enhance free choice by providing information, by removing personal and interpersonal barriers to it, by alleviating anxiety, to allow our clients to see the full ramifications of all their decisions. To do this, we must help them walk the tightrope between independence and connectedness, to feel individually authorized to conduct their lives as they choose, while at the same time acknowledging that they are part of a larger system, a family, an ethnic group, a culture. To which do we owe our allegiance and how do we choose among them? These are the questions of our time, and helping people find answers to them is the true goal of any psychotherapy.

A SYSTEMS MODEL FOR INTERMARRIAGE

It was Kurt Lewin who said, "There is nothing so practical as a good theory." Systems theory, or family systems theory, allows the clinician to help in a way that supports both individual autonomy and interpersonal interconnectedness.

Parameters of the Systemic Model

Autonomy and interconnectedness. Whatever clinical model we adopt, it must allow us to be therapeutic, to provide help to the people who seek clinical services. In medicine, if a patient recovers after a treatment, then the treatment is therapeutic regardless of how the patient feels about what was done to him or her. In psychotherapy, there is no outcome independent of how the client feels, and the client is the ultimate judge of whether a therapeutic approach or technique has been successful. Yet by what criterion does the therapist or the client judge outcome? Help must be more than encouraging one to feel good, or else unmitigated praise would be therapeutic, and while some would call it necessary (Rogers 1951), it is not sufficient. Help must be more than encouraging selfishness, otherwise the social value of psychotherapy would be open to question. We have returned to our question of values, to confront again the question, What are the proper goals of psychotherapy? While admitting that these may differ somewhat from therapist to therapist and from school to school, I endorse the values that I have suggested in my previous writings (Sirkin and Rueveni 1992; Sirkin and Wynne 1990): *To maximize both individual autonomy and interpersonal interconnectedness*, to encourage clients to walk the fine line between the two but never one to the exclusion of the other. No person is an island, but at the same time, every person needs functional boundaries.

Family as the patient. Another parameter of the systemic model is an appreciation of the system as a whole, not one part to the exclusion of the others (Satir 1964; Watzlawick, Weakland, and Fisch 1974). The goal is to help the entire family system when possible, not simply to fix the presenting problem (child). This systemic view is one of the strengths of the model, and it encourages the clinician to redefine the problem in a way that includes all family members. This parameter also encourages family members to find solutions to their problems that are as acceptable as possible to the maximum number of family members. The win-lose mentality so common in family "gamesmanship" needs to be replaced with a win-win or compromise mentality. While no solution to a family's problem may make everyone happy, the best solutions accommodate the most people.

Respect for religious values. Jewish agencies and clinicians, in addition to the parameters mentioned above, must also be halachically sensitive. They work within a Jewish framework that they should neither apologize for nor ignore. At the same time, the professional role of the psychotherapist precludes foisting our opinions and values onto our clients. Again, this is where we differ from rabbis, whose professional role is to represent those values. For example, if a religious Jew tells his rabbi he is considering eating a lobster, the rabbi's role would be to remind him that such foods are not kosher. If the religious Jew tells his psychotherapist the same thing, the therapist would strive to help the individual understand the motivations, and the intrapsychic and interpersonal ramifications, of such an act. It would not be appropriate for the therapist to tell the client not to eat such foods, despite the religious and personal sensitivities of the therapist.

Characteristics of the Systemic Model

Family systems theory represents a complex set of ideas that encompasses numerous schools and a variety of distinct approaches (Hoffman 1981). It would not be appropriate, for the purposes of this paper, to present a thorough overview of these theories. Rather, I will present for the clinician working with intermarriage a set of guidelines based on systems concepts that I have found extremely practical.

Work with any part of the system. In systems parlance, any subsystem is isomorphic to the whole, meaning that the patterns of the whole system are present in any part of the system. To insist on working with only one part of the system, e.g., the potential intermarrier, is to lose an opportunity to impact the system as a whole, e.g., through the parents or siblings. From a practical standpoint, often the parents are the first, sometimes the only, part of the system that presents itself for treatment. The clinician should work with any subsystem that presents itself, both to impact on that subsystem and to impact on the system as a whole.

Strengthen boundaries. No system is viable unless it has viable boundaries. The ideal boundary is semipermeable, it contains what is inside it while at the same time allowing information to cross it. Each person in a family is a subsystem that needs strong, semipermeable boundaries. The parental couple in the system also needs strong but permeable boundaries. A system without strong boundaries will fall apart, but a system with impermeable boundaries will ultimately deteriorate. Families in trouble often have a confused sense of boundaries (Boss and Greenberg 1984).

Encourage communication across boundaries. This is the complement to strengthening boundaries. Living systems are open systems that allow information to be exchanged across the boundary. One of the essential features of any systemic therapy is the encouragement of communication across boundaries. This exchange of information can strengthen subsystems and the identity of the system as a whole (Reiss 1981).

Discourage cutoffs. Human systems are sometimes characterized by cutoffs which represent a total breakdown of communication. These are often present in families where one member, or side, has barely talked to another member, or side, in years. The ultimate cutoff is when a parent sits *shiva* for a child who behaves in a way of which the parent disapproves. System problems are often irreparable while cutoffs are in place, and they prevent a system from functioning as a healthy whole (Bowen 1978).

Expand the system. The solutions to family problems are often found by expanding the system to include other family subsystems. Intractable arguments can often be resolved, or at least refocused, by including people who were not part of the original argument. For example, an ongoing disagreement between par-

ent and child may be changed by including a grandparent.
Expanding the system allows the therapist to incorporate other
perspectives from the same family without taking sides (Speck
and Attneave 1973).

Recognize key family values. It is remarkable that an endeavor
such as psychotherapy, which deals so often with people's values,
has so little to say about the topic of values. It is almost as if there
were a trade secret, i.e., everyone knows therapy is about values
but no one wants to say so because it opens a pandora's box of
questions with no easy answers: Which values? Whose values?
Why those values and not other values? Although the precise
definition of "family" may differ among sociologists, economists,
anthropologists, etc., I want to suggest that from the inside, from
within the family's perspective, it is a core set of values that
defines the family.

American Jewish families share a core set of human values
(Herz and Rosen 1982; Linzer 1984). The Jewish religion itself
comprises an important set of communal values. These values,
such as communal worship, communal charity, and dietary and
marriage customs, have strengthened the Jewish community *qua*
community. Other key values are operative at the personal, family, and social levels: the importance of tolerance, equality of
opportunity, and social justice; the value of family life; the importance of education. These are the major themes, heard to a
greater or lesser degree in most Jewish families, that comprise the
symphony of values for Jews in America today. Intermarriage,
depending on how the other themes are orchestrated in any given
family, may either sound a highly discordant note or be a coun-
terpoint in a melody that sounds like modern American assimilation.

The Therapist's Multiple Roles

Consistent with the family systems approach, it is incumbent
upon the therapist to be flexible in his or her approach to inter-

marriage. There can be no simple "cookbook" or "how-to" guide for the clinician working with these families. Within the family therapy literature, however, a number of metaframeworks emerge which help to guide the clinician faced with the family problem of intermarriage.

Therapist as system consultant. The consultant's relationship to the family differs somewhat from the therapist's. While some would argue that this is only a matter of degree, that all therapeutic relationships are essentially consultative, there are important differences. In their important work on this subject, McDaniel, Weber, and Wynne (1986) note that "consultation provides a relationship in which the family and the consultant can collaboratively delineate the problem and consider options for resolution. . . . [Whereas] the therapist takes direct and primary responsibility for facilitating change . . . the consultee, not the consultant, retains explicit responsibility for change" (p. 17). The initial phase of any work with families struggling with intermarriage should be seen as consultation, not therapy. This gives everyone in the system, including the potential therapist, time to evaluate the many variables involved and to collaborate on a course of work together that will maximally meet the family's needs.

Multidirectional partiality. Although multidirectional partiality may be little known beyond the work of Boszormenyi-Nagy (Boszormenyi-Nagy and Spark 1973), I consider it the single most essential tool for the therapist/consultant in cases of intermarriage. Multidirectional partiality is defined as "an attitude that allows a therapist to empathize with each family member, to recognize the merits of each, and to take sides because of these merits" (Simon, Stierlin, and Wynne 1985, p. 232). It is this capacity that prevents the therapist from taking sides and from favoring one individual or subsystem in the therapy session over another. The therapist must maintain the technical freedom and empathic flexibility to side with different family members at different times in a session.

The psychoeducational component. Many family therapists are finding that there is a need to educate the families that come to them about the very nature of the problems for which they are seeking help (Anderson, Hogarty, and Reiss 1980). As with consultation, it may be argued that all therapy has a component of education in it, and this may be. In the case of intermarriage, however, there are facts about Jewish identity (Gordis and Ben-Horin, 1991), intermarriage (Mayer 1985; Schneider 1989), and the changing role of religion throughout the life-cycle (Fowler 1981) that should be part of any discussion.

Engaging the question of Jewish identity. Like a haunting melody that one can't seem to shake, the question of Jewish identity lies lurking in the background for every family struggling with problems of intermarriage. What does it mean to be Jewish? What are the core components of Jewish identity? What are the peripheral components of Jewish identity? Most parents approach professional help for problems related to intermarriage intent on having the professional raise these issues with their children, while most young adults contemplating intermarriage usually prefer to put these questions on the "back burner" or to deny their importance. Yet the question of Jewish identity lies at the heart of a family's objections to intermarriage. The very possibility forces everyone in the family to ask themselves a most difficult question: What does it mean to *me* to be Jewish, and how will this potential intermarriage affect me? This can actually be a frightening question for Jews who do not understand the strength or tentativeness of their connection to Judaism. It is incumbent upon the therapist to ask the question again and again until each and every family member has struggled with it.

TECHNICAL ISSUES IN THE CLINICAL
TREATMENT OF INTERMARRIAGE

In the first part of this essay, the framework was set for understanding the clinical impact of intermarriage on Jewish families as well as some of the ethical dilemmas that might confront a worker or therapist dealing with these issues in the clinic. The outlines of a theoretical approach utilizing some of the basic tenets of family systems theory was also suggested. I will now elaborate more fully some of the technical issues involved in treatment.

FAMILY–DYSTONIC INTERMARRIAGE

It must be reiterated from the outset that the fact of intermarriage or the impending possibility of intermarriage is not in itself a clinical condition requiring treatment. Millions of people in the United States alone intermarry without incident, and the rate is on the increase (Spickard 1989). It is only when intermarriage creates significant family distress for which counseling is sought that it warrants the label "family-dystonic."[2] This term was first introduced in clinical work with families by Bruce Grellong and myself in our work with Jewish cult-involved families (Sirkin and Grellong 1988): "Although cult involvement may be fully ego-syntonic for the involved individual, it may be dystonic for the rest of the family system. That is, family members, especially parents, may experience great distress when relationships are strained or ties broken due to involvement in extremist groups" (p. 3).

While I am *not* suggesting that intermarriage is the same as joining a destructive cult, I do think that some families experience the proposition with equal disquietude. In fact, the treatment model that I am suggesting in the present paper is an extension of the work I have done with family-dystonic problems related to cult involvement (Sirkin 1990) and folie à deux (Sirkin and Rueveni 1992).

Common Denominators in Intermarriage-Dystonic Families

The family life-cycle. The family life-cycle is a developmental schema that allows clinicians to view families not as static but as everchanging, multiperson organisms that dance through time (Carter and McGoldrick 1989). When an individual reaches a point in the individual life-cycle when he or she is ready for marriage (Erikson 1950), this signals that the family too must prepare for both loss and gain (McCullough and Rutenberg 1989). Sometimes referred to as "launching," this stage involves the loss of a family member due to marriage but also the need to include spouse and in-laws in a redefinition of extended family. There is a special stress on parents at this stage, especially when the last child is contemplating marriage. The parental couple has achieved a balance, of sorts, that involves sharing the multiple responsibilities of raising children.

A redefinition of the marriage, and the couple's relationship to each other, faces the parents whose last child is leaving home. When an intermarriage is a possibility, this may give the parents one last crisis to unite around and thereby avoid an often painful renegotiation of the marital relationship.

CASE 1: Sylvia and Don had two children, Lisa and Michael. They had not had a happy marriage but remained together for the sake of the children and "financial reasons." They came for help because Michael was contemplating marrying a woman, his second marriage, who was not Jewish. Upon talking to Michael, it became clear that he had no intention of remarrying so soon after his divorce and that his parents' constant harping was actually pushing him closer to marriage than he wanted to be. The parents were urged to give Michael some space. They then presented their concerns about Lisa, who was married to an Israeli whom they disapproved of and who was abusive to her. Lisa clearly rejected her parents' efforts to "help" her and insisted that she felt satisfied in her marriage. When the therapy turned to

Sylvia and Don's relationship, the sessions became bitter and acrimonious. They finally decided they were not suited to each other and began separation proceedings after thirty-three years of marriage.

Religion may also take on different meanings for people at different stages of the life-cycle. Fowler (1981) notes that people become more religious as they get older. While religion may be an important issue for parents, it may be less important for their children as young adults. We will return to this issue when counseling interfaith couples, but at this point it is important to realize that it may be an important difference within families between generations.

Multigenerational issues. Bowen's (1978) family system theory stresses the multigenerational nature of many family problems and conflicts. Unresolved issues in one generation often become the sources for unresolved problems in the next generation. In a brilliant article entitled, "The Myth of the Shiksa," Ed Friedman, a rabbi and family therapist who was a student of Bowen's, discusses the multigenerational processes at work in many cases of severe conflict about intermarriage (Friedman 1982). Although Friedman, in his discussion, ignores some of the real problems that intermarriage may pose, he nevertheless identifies some of the common distortions that can occur.

Boundary issues. The centrality of family in Jewish life (Herz and Rosen 1982), and the resultant intensity of relationships in Jewish families, often leads to boundary distortions. Within the family, boundaries may be poorly formed and very porous, often resulting in enmeshment (Minuchin 1974). One need only picture the classic image of Mrs. Portnoy standing at the bathroom door inquiring about her adolescent son's bowels, to understand the extent to which interpersonal boundaries may be violated.

Almost as a counterbalance, the boundary between the family and the outside world, especially the non-Jewish world, can be very rigid and highly impermeable. For families with inflexible boundaries even an ordinary marriage may be difficult. Intermarriage becomes nearly an impossibility. If nothing else, intermarriage issues are boundary issues.

CASE 2: Mrs. Pizerofsky talked in uncertain terms about her daughter's recent wedding. She and her husband had sought consultation over a year earlier because of their concern that their daughter was dating a non-Jew. After a year of consultation at the Beren Center, she broke off the relationship and had recently married a Jewish young man. I was puzzled at the mother's lack of enthusiasm. It turned out that the young man, in the mother's opinion, was difficult to get along with. He insisted that the daughter move to another borough of the city where they had found an apartment. And she couldn't understand why the young man should object if she spoke to her daughter several times a day. That her daughter was revealing intimate details of their sex life, upon which this mother felt free to comment not only to her new son-in-law, but to his mother, did not initially seem problematic to her. With some coaching from the therapist, Mr. Pizerofsky was able to convince his wife that without some restraint she would be jeopardizing her relationship with her new in-laws.

Individual issues. Families experiencing family-dystonic intermarriage problems are often caught in a power struggle. The individual considering the marriage is faced with a dilemma: me vs. my family of origin, my way vs. my family's way, to go forward vs. to go backward. The parents often frame the dilemma in terms of gratitude vs. ingratitude or respect vs. disrespect. These frames for the problem are unhelpful primarily because they do not encompass the reality of all the participants. Intermarriage is not always (or even usually) a matter of disrespect or ingratitude toward one's parents (Sirkin 1993). Neither is the ability to hear one's parents' concerns a case of "caving in to them" or a lack of independence. The proper goal of treatment is to help families by helping the individuals in them negotiate the delicate balance between autonomy and interdependence. Like sailing between Scylla and Charybdis, it may not be easy, but psychological survival depends on it.

Presenting Problems

Family therapists, since the inception of this type of therapy, have noted that the presenting problem is often an indication of a disturbed pattern of family relations (Vogel and Bell 1960). For a family therapist to treat only the identified patient (IP) would be like a medical doctor controlling a fever but doing nothing for the underlying infection.

Experience at the Beren Center indicates that in most cases of family-dystonic intermarriage, the parents will contact the clinic presenting the adult child as the "problem." At the first interview, it is important to hear how, specifically, the IP is described. Is he or she portrayed as confused, rebellious, ungrateful, disturbed, or uncaring about Judaism and/or family? It is here we begin to sense the themes that may be acted out around the intermarriage. In extreme cases, the IP is described as a potential parent killer, as in statements such as, "Since this whole situation began, my heart condition has worsened," or "I don't think his mother/ father will survive the shock if s/he goes through with this." Although such statements may sound like rhetorical hyperbole, they nevertheless express the deep pain of family members.

Sometimes the conflict in the family is not focused on the child who is intermarrying but between the spouses. This may be seen as a "perverse triangle" in which a child and parent join forces against the other parent (Haley 1967). The spouse who takes the religious "high ground" by opposing the intermarriage sees the other parent as deficient in some moral or religious way. The more "liberal" parent often views the disapproving spouse as unreasonable and rigid. Such couples may need several sessions together to sort out these feelings before involving the child in the treatment.

The interfaith couple themselves may at times seek help. Common problems for these couples often derive from some slippage of an uneasy truce that was achieved at an earlier point in the relationship.

CASE 3: A Christian man married a Jewish woman, assuring her that they would only celebrate Jewish holidays in the home. By the third year of marriage, with a two-year-old in the house, he decided he missed a Christmas tree and that it wouldn't hurt if he introduced a small one into the home. His wife felt betrayed but also noted how much pleasure the tree gave him. The following year, the tree was a little bigger and his wife was in a quandary. The negotiations and renegotiations in interfaith marriages are endless.

These couples tend to experience more problems around the times of key life-cycle stages or events: the birth of a child, the beginning of religious training, when the children reach Bar or Bat Mitzvah age.

Sometimes an individual, by him- or herself, will seek help to sort out problems related to an impending intermarriage. I have found that it is usually helpful to meet the potential spouse at some point in this process, although not always right away. A relationship should first be established with the person seeking help. The person who comes alone may resist bringing in the partner for one of two reasons. Either they do not want to alienate the partner by expressing doubts openly to a third party or they want pointers on how to overcome potential problems without involving the partner at all. Such cases are usually more similar to individual therapy than family systems therapy, although there will always be significant overlap.

Clinical Goals

In earlier sections of this paper, I suggested a general outline of a family systems approach to working with intermarriage-related problems. In this section, I will discuss the specific application of these general principles.

Consultation before treatment. Consultation is not simply a set of skills, it is a mind-set. I have come to believe that clinicians, before engaging in a course of psychotherapeutic treatment, should begin as consultants to the system. This is especially true for problems such as intermarriage, because they are not typically associated with psychotherapeutic intervention. Sometimes the distinction is subtle, but it is important nevertheless. The consultant tries to get an overview of all the variables in a situation, determines possible courses of action, then makes recommendations. One such recommendation may be a course of family counseling or couple counseling, or a referral to a rabbi. The consultant relationship provides maximum flexibility, while the therapeutic relationship, in contrast, already makes certain assumptions that may be constraining. The goal of the consultation is to determine what action to take that is mutually agreeable to the professional and all involved members of the system. A consultation may take one, two, or three sessions, or in some cases can take place over the telephone.

CASE 4: The caller asked if this was where they stopped intermarriage. I replied that we were a clinic and counseled people about intermarriage, but that ultimately the individual had to choose for him- or herself. She seemed momentarily confused, then asked, "But isn't this a Jewish clinic?" I assured her it was but that our approach was psychological and not strictly religious. We discussed her personal situation, but she was adamant about the need for a religiously oriented individual to speak to her son in religious terms. She was referred to a rabbi.

This was a situation where the individual was not really interested in the type of services we offered. It would have been potentially unethical to begin a course of treatment with her, or her son, without her understanding what we were offering and what we were not offering.

Psychoeducation. The psychoeducational approach takes into account that there is specific knowledge that may be helpful to families and individuals trying to cope with an illness or problem. This knowledge complements therapeutic interventions. Information specific to intermarriage falls into three categories: risk factors, issues related to children, and issues related to self. In terms of risk, it is a fact that the divorce rate is much greater for intermarriage than for Jewish in-marriage (Mayer 1985). These risks are significantly reduced in conversionary marriages. Also, intermarriage rates are much higher for divorced people than for first-time marriages. Children raised with a dual religious identity will have a minimal sense of Jewish identity (Medding et al. 1992). The Jewish partner in an intermarriage also limits his or her potential for enhanced Jewish identity: "mixed-marriage must be regarded as a virtual bar to the achievement of a high level of Jewish identification" (Medding, et al. 1992, p. 37). This may be especially problematic when one realizes that religion becomes more important as one grows into middle and late adulthood (Fowler 1981). In other words, couples should be made aware of psychological research that indicates that differences that are not important in their twenties may become more important in their thirties, forties, fifties, and beyond. Perhaps this is one factor that explains the high divorce rate among inter-marrieds.

CASE 5: The caller asked if this was where they stopped intermarriage. I replied that we were a clinic and that we counseled people about intermarriage, but that ultimately the individual had to choose for him- or herself. The caller seemed relieved, expressing his concern due to the fact that we were, after all, a Jewish organization. This turned out to be a caller who was considering intermarriage himself and wanted to have all the facts and data so he could make an informed decision. We met several times, first with him alone, and then with his partner, to discuss some of the facts I had, and some of the concerns both of them had.

Enhance communication. An integral part of any family treatment is to enhance communication within subsystems and within the system as a whole. Each of the parents must be clear where the other stands on the important issues, e.g., meeting the boyfriend/girlfriend, supporting the marriage, attending the wedding, paying for the wedding, etc. It is only by discussing their feelings and values about these issues that the parental couple can feel united in their position toward the intermarriage.

Paradoxically, communication across subsystem boundaries may serve to strengthen those boundaries and thereby benefit the family as a whole. Parents are encouraged to state their feelings to their children as strongly as they deem appropriate. It is vital to the work of the therapy that the therapist not communicate for the parents, or in place of the parents, but encourage the parents to communicate directly to their child. But communication, at its best, is a two-way street, and parents must be helped to listen to their children. Adult children must be encouraged to articulate their needs and feelings, which then become the basis for an ongoing dialogue between parents and child. Sometimes siblings will have something important to add to this dialogue and should be encouraged to do so.

Articulate individual values. Clinical experience teaches that most people believe that they behave in a manner that is self-consistent. That is, people seem to believe that they operate from a consistent set of values; they engage in activities and object to activities based on those values. What are the values that parents wish to articulate in their opposition to intermarriage? What are the values that young people seek to affirm when they inter-marry? The articulation of individual values is essential for the differentiation that is one criterion of healthy family functioning (Bowen 1978).

Sometimes the values people hold are mutually incompatible, and it is here that therapy can often be quite helpful. The desire to intermarry (without conversion of the non-Jewish spouse) and the desire to have Jewishly identified children may be incompati-ble values, according to the available research (Medding et al. 1992). Not that a person cannot want both things, but the facts are that they do not occur together. Sometimes strongly held val-ues lead to conflicting choices that can be postponed but rarely avoided.

Relate individual and system values. Individuals do not function in a vacuum. Individuals are members of larger systems, i.e., fam-ilies and religious and ethnic groups. These larger systems also have values that impose themselves on individuals. When people choose to associate, or become (or remain) members of these larger systems, they must constantly work to maintain some con-sistent connection between the individual system of the self and the larger family or social system. This does not mean that indi-viduals are slavishly committed to following the dictates of the group. In the healthiest systems, there is room for dialogue and flexibility. Within limits, some systems can change. This is the purpose of communication and the hope of therapy.

CASE 6: Sam and his wife, Minna, called me for an appoint-ment as soon as possible. Unlike most callers, who want to know a bit about the Center before scheduling a meeting, they had been referred by their rabbi and that was good enough for them; and besides, they were desperate people. Both Sam and Minna were intent on "saving" Saul, their only son, from the horrific fate that he had planned for himself and his entire family. They were an Orthodox family that, they assured me, had done all the "right" things. They were observant, they sent their children to yeshivas, these kinds of things weren't supposed to happen to people like them. I was the last in a long line of counselors the father and mother had sought advice from and the first secular advisor (i.e., I wasn't a rabbi or a rebbetzin).

Saul, their son, was a 27-year-old young man, in his fourth year of medical school at an upstate medical college. He was the middle child, with an older sister who was single and a nurse, and a younger sister, who was attending a women's yeshiva in Israel. His parents were not originally from observant families and his maternal uncle was Reform; the uncle's daughter, Saul's cousin, had recently married a non-Jew. Saul had also attended yeshivas during his adolescence and college. During his first year of medical school, Saul met an Oriental woman who was not Jewish. They had been dating for about three years and were apparently intending marriage. The parents had found out about the relationship about a year ago and had done everything to discourage it, from begging to berating and everything in-between. They refused to meet the girlfriend.

As the meanings of this potential intermarriage were being explored for Sam and Minna, one thing became clear. In addition to the feelings of failure and betrayal that are common in such families, another theme emerged very clearly: shame. As we talked about their objections to the intermarriage, they mentioned in passing that Saul had assured them that his girlfriend would undergo an Orthodox conversion. When I suggested that this must have been quite a relief for them, Sam looked at me wide-eyed and said, "But Doctor, you don't understand, we will never accept this girl, she's not like us, she's not our kind, no conversion will change that." As we discussed the issue further, my fears were confirmed: this was not about religion or halacha; it was prejudice, pure and simple.

"Of course my son thinks we're racists," the father added.

Upon meeting Saul, first privately and then with his parents, it turned out that his fiancée was indeed studying with an Orthodox rabbi and was intent on converting. My work with this family consisted of helping the parents to see that their rejection of the fiancée was not grounded in the values they professed to endorse. Their son did indeed support many of his family's religious values, if not their prejudice against other racial groups. Their values compelled them to accept this convert, and they realized they had much more to lose than gain by their continued opposition.

Maintain multidirected partiality. Multidirected partiality is not just a technique, it is a philosophy of treatment grounded in an abiding respect for all members of a system and their values (Boszormenyi-Nagy and Spark 1973). It refers to the therapist's "freedom to take turns in siding with one family member after another as his [*sic*] empathic understanding and technical leverage require" (Boszormenyi-Nagy and Spark 1973, p. 179). Besides being an important value, multidirected partiality makes strategic sense. Why would someone in a family come for a consultation or treatment with a professional whom they believed would take sides against them? In order to join with every member of the system, it is important for the therapist to demonstrate an understanding of each member's unique perspective on the problem and unique position in the family system (Minuchin and Fishman 1981). The skills to achieve this may leave a therapist feeling insincere or the parents feeling betrayed by a therapist they thought "understood" them. But it is also a method that models mutual respect, open communication, and genuine dialogue between people. It is an essential quality for anyone who desires to do clinical work with families struggling with family-dystonic intermarriage issues.

WORKING WITH SUBSYSTEMS

The essence of the systemic approach is the view that intermarriage, at least family-dystonic intermarriage, is not simply about one person's decision to marry. The potential event that is giving rise to family dystonia must be understood in the context of the entire family system. In the typical clinical situation, however, it is rare for the entire family to present itself at the clinician's door, eager for treatment. The reality is that first contact, initial consultation, and sometimes the entire treatment take place with only a subsystem of the entire family system. Each subsystem approaches the clinic with characteristic concerns which must be understood by the clinician in the context of the entire system.

Parents

Our data suggest that approximately 90 percent of all our contacts come from distressed parents who have an adult child contemplating intermarriage. Some calls come from extended family (aunts, uncles, brothers, sisters) who are requesting help. Often parents are uncertain about the kind of help offered, sometimes they are even uncertain about what they want to do.

The initial goals of the early session(s) are to help the parents articulate their individual concerns. They may feel that their concerns about the intermarriage are obvious, but the fact is that mothers and fathers often have different concerns. Try to have them be clear about religious considerations versus family comfort versus concern for their children versus apprehension about grandchildren. Often all of these anxieties relate directly or indirectly to issues of Jewish identity and continuity. Explore the vicissitudes of Jewish identity in the life of each individual and in their family life as well, i.e., since they became parents.

Most family systems therapists use genograms in their work (Guerin and Pendagast 1976). Genograms, maps of the family system, are invaluable as a tool to gather information, join with the system, and keep track of the players. When constructing genograms in cases of family-dystonic intermarriage, explore such themes as Jewish identity, Jewish involvements, religious observance, and incidences of intermarriage in the extended family. Relationships with the IP should be noted to understand the role that this person, and his or her intermarriage, might be playing in the dynamics of the family system.

The clinician should attempt to differentiate between "healthy" agendas and "unhealthy" agendas and, when possible, emphasize the former. Of course, the terms "healthy" and "unhealthy" are value judgments, but I have in mind situations such as those described in Case 6. Most opposition to intermarriage is part xenophobia and part affirmation of positive Jewish values. It is the positive values which are ultimately the most robust and have the greatest potential to impact the system positively.

In family-dystonic situations, the potential intermarriage will often stress a couple's relationship along previously established stress lines. Tried-and-true themes from old arguments often reemerge (e.g., fathers are too hard on sons and mothers too soft, vice versa with daughters, etc.). As in the example of Case 1, the disagreements about intermarriage may mask other conflicts. These conflicts must be explored and to some degree settled, or at least put aside, in order to deal with the problems around the intermarriage.

At some point the therapeutic work with parents must involve an exploration of possible futures. What if the intermarriage takes place? How will the parents handle their relationships with their intermarried child, the spouse, their other children? These questions are by no means meant as subtle encouragement to accept the intermarriage, for whether or not to do so is ultimately each parent's choice. But thinking about the limits to which they will go in opposition to the intermarriage allows subsequent discussions with their child to proceed on a firm footing.

CASE 7: Abe and Dinah contacted the Beren Center from their home in California. This modern Orthodox couple had just received the devastating news that their oldest daughter, a professional living in the Midwest, was engaged to be married to a Christian man. To add insult to injury, she had decided to convert to Christianity. No matter what they tried, their daughter would not reconsider her decision, nor would she meet with a family therapist. Her ultimatum to them was to accept her decision and come to the wedding or risk being alienated from her. With professional help, the parents decided they could in no way support their daughter's decision by attending the wedding. They allowed their other two daughters the freedom to choose to go or not. One daughter attended, the other did not. The daughter who attended was "traumatized," according to the parents, and will no longer have anything to do with her sister. There is now little contact between the married daughter and her family of origin, but her parents feel they acted consistently with their long held values and do not regret their actions. They have since become active members in their community to help Jewish singles meet.

Individuals Contemplating Intermarriage

The individual contemplating intermarriage is at an important developmental point in his or her life. Particularly in family-dystonic situations, these individuals are forced to dramatically assess the positives and negatives of close family ties and the alternatives. In my opinion, the individual who seeks help, or agrees to help, without the partner is struggling with different issues than someone who comes with the partner. These issues usually have more to do with relationships to family of origin than with relationships to the potential partner. Because the partner has been excluded, the focus of the work naturally falls more to the individual.

Individual work with someone contemplating intermarriage may be very similar to psychotherapy for other presenting problems. Of course, even systemic therapists work with individuals but do not allow themselves to lose sight of the family context (Aylmer 1989). The issues related to intermarriage may surface in a variety of ways. For example, the individual may be struggling with parents about closeness, career, or religion in general without specific reference to the potential intermarriage. The individual may be struggling with his or her own feelings about religion, children, career, or family. It is useful to explore how someone's struggle or ambivalences about religion are often played out in the interfaith relationship. One hypothesis about these relationships is that they are an acting-out of one's ambivalence toward Judaism, in all of its forms, e.g., religious, social, familial. As with any other form of acting-out, when all the related feelings can be verbalized and explored, the need to act-out diminishes. This is not to say that all interfaith relationships and marriages are a form of acting-out, but when they are, individual psychotherapy will be helpful.

The exploration of potential futures is useful for these individuals. Where they expect religion to fit in to their future family lives and what they want their potential spouses to know about Judaism are just some of the questions that can be explored. One of the ironies of intermarriage is that someone who believes religion is not important is often forced to represent and teach and instill the values of religion in his or her future family. This often comes as a surprise to someone who expected to be "escaping" religious demands. The salience of religion in the sessions will vary from person to person and from time to time throughout the treatment relationship.

CASE 8: The rebbetzin of an ultra-Orthodox synagogue contacted the Center about her niece, Roberta, who was dating a non-Jewish boy. Both parents and extended family were quite upset. The parents, who were nominally Orthodox, contacted me and came in for a consultation. They brought Roberta to the following session. The outcome of these sessions was that she was willing to meet with me, in individual therapy, to explore her relationship, but she did not want to include the parents. Individual psychotherapy proceeded, although her boyfriend came in with her on two occasions.

The treatment with Roberta has been ongoing for almost two years. The focus on issues related to her boyfriend, whom she had wanted to marry, receded, and issues with her parents and family came to the fore. Although she resisted repeated attempts to have her parents come in to sessions, the work has progressed nevertheless. When the break-up with the boyfriend came, Roberta became suicidal and was seen twice a week for a period of months. She continues to be seen weekly to work on issues that are typical for someone in her mid-twenties. Discussions about religion may occur periodically in the context of talking about her family or new men in her life, but they are rarely the focus of treatment.

The Couple

When a couple comes in together, especially for the first session, this usually indicates that there is a strong commitment to remain together. By appearing together they are making a public statement of sorts that they want to be seen as a couple. The initial consultations must be used to assess the couple's commitment to each other, each person's investment in working on issues that may be difficult for them, and how important religious differences may be to each of them and to their families of origin. Three-generational genograms for each person will assist the therapist in tracking some of these issues.

Couples will present with varying degrees of sophistication with regard to the difficulties they will face. Some approach the thought of potential problems with massive denial, truly believing that none of the statistics will apply to them. Some may try to prepare for future problems by exacting promises from each other, as with the couple in Case 3. The most sanguine situations are those in which both members of the couple understand that the consistent expectation of ongoing discussions and renegotiations is the only protection they will ever have.

Experience has taught that couples at different stages of involvement have different needs. A couple at the dating stage has the most flexibility in terms of a final commitment, and both members of the couple are relatively free to reconsider every aspect of the relationship, including marriage. These couples need to understand the significant problems they will face and begin to develop a sense of how willing their partner will be to negotiate differences and how much room there is for compromise. Couples who are engaged have already made a commitment to each other and are therefore less flexible. This diminished flexibility may push a couple toward denial or trivialization of problems. It will facilitate the counseling to have couples agree to hold off on any marriage plans until after the counseling process is completed, or at least to commit to a hiatus in the planning. This may also help parents feel less anxious and allow them to participate in some of the work.

There is a growing body of clinical dialogue about therapy for interfaith couples. McGoldrick and Garcia-Preto (1984) discuss some of the generic issues relevant to this work, while Perel (1990) and Crohn (1986) discuss some of the issues especially relevant for Jews who intermarry. The essence of this work lies in helping each member come to terms with the realization that their spouse comes from a different background, with different ground rules and different expectations. Again, an acceptance of the ongoing need for discussion of these differences is the first step in the therapy process (Petsonk 1990).

The common difficulties that arise in these relationships can be summarized in three words: Christmas, conversion, and kids.

The issue of Christmas simply cannot be avoided in American interfaith families. Every year the culture reminds these families that someone (or some people) in their home is not part of the mainstream religious culture. Christian family members may experience a longing for familiar rituals, while many Jews feel secretly threatened or alienated during this time (Sirkin 1992). Even when the couple reach a truce, families of origin may exert pulls that create additional tensions.

Conversion becomes an issue periodically when it seems to be the only protection against the dissolution of Jewish identity that many intermarried people experience (Cowan and Cowan 1987). Because American culture is, for the most part, Christian, the issue of conversion is often more pressing for the Jewish partner, as some modicum of protection from the forces of assimilation. Often the issue of conversion is broached early in the relationship, though tentatively, then dropped like a hot potato if the non-Jewish spouse resists. It may come up at various points in the life-cycle, such as the birth of a child, at age six or seven, when most children begin religious training, or around the time of the Bar or Bat Mitzvah. Religious conversion is the only obvious way to settle some of the Jewish identity concerns that arise from intermarriage.

Conversion of the spouse is closely related to the issue of the religious identity of children. A couple may agree early on that the children will be raised as Jewish, but rarely do they ask how a non-Jew can participate in the raising of Jewish children. Unless he or she has made a commitment to learn about Jewish beliefs, rituals, and customs, the non-Jewish parent will often feel alienated from certain parts of family life. Some couples compromise on this issue by raising children with exposure to both traditions or to none (Petsonk and Remsen 1988). These parents must realize that this is a formula for raising non-Jewish children (Medding et al. 1992) with the added potential for identity confusion and lower self-esteem (Phinney 1990).

This section cannot conclude without a brief discussion of the difficulties of the traditional Jew, or Jewish agency, in the counseling of people who are already intermarried. Jewish law is quite clear in its nonacceptance of intermarriage. The task of helping an intermarried couple to improve their relationship in order to remain intermarried poses an ethical dilemma for the traditional Jew. This is one reason why some halachically oriented therapists will only counsel individuals or couples prior to intermarriage. There are different attitudes among different denominations within Judaism that could justify a multitude of approaches. The only clear guidelines for the therapist are to be aware of his or her own position, and then to communicate that position to supervisors, colleagues, and patients, when appropriate.

Support Groups

A new trend in group psychotherapy is the advent of time-limited, focused groups for particular problems (MacKenzie 1992). There is a significant overlap between these groups and the type of groups offered by family-life education services through Jewish Family Services and Jewish community centers. The latter usually have a more psychoeducational orientation around Jewish issues, although all groups share common aspects of the group process.

Couple-support groups were pioneered by the Union of American Hebrew Congregations in the late 1970s. These groups are open to couples both married and considering marriage. Tending to be time-limited, with a heavy educational component for the non-Jewish partner, these groups provide a forum for couples to exchange opinions, frustrations, and information. Some couples form lasting friendships with other couples. These groups are currently sponsored on local levels by Jewish Family Services, Jewish community centers, and individual synagogues, primarily Reform synagogues but a growing number of Conservative synagogues as well.

Parent-support groups are probably the fastest-growing service to this population. Many of the parents who seek support would place themselves in the family-dystonic category, although some are simply seeking more information. As discussed, these groups are often helpful in sorting out significant differences between parents.

One criticism of these groups is that they usually mix potential intermarriers with those who have already intermarried. Likewise, parent groups are also usually mixed. My experience has been that premarriage and postmarriage individuals are distinct, with different salient issues for each. The tendency to mix the two often means that some participants, usually the premarriage ones, are inadvertently silenced. For example, a subgroup of parents discussing their concerns about their interdating children might want to focus on their fears, their anger, and prevention of the marriage. A subgroup of parents whose children have already intermarried will tend to focus on forgiveness, acceptance, and making grandchildren more Jewish. The latter parents often feel threatened by the anger and fear of the former and seek to reassure them by telling them that everything will be all right and that there is family life after intermarriage. This is not what the premarriage parents want to hear and it is often not helpful for them. Similarly, working with couples who are struggling with intermarriage often creates a "jump in—the water's fine" atmosphere that makes it harder for couples to reconsider what is, at best, a difficult life choice.

CASE 9: A young psychologist was contacted by a Conservative synagogue to run a group for the parents of intermarried and interdating couples. The original group leader, an older woman who was intermarried herself, was retiring, so they were willing to try a young unknown. Membership in the group would be open, not just to synagogue members but to the community. The rabbi and the temple president planned to attend the first meeting, despite the fact that there was no intermarriage or interdating in their families. Although it was suggested to them that their presence might not be helpful, it seems that temple politics dictated otherwise. Thirty-one people arrived for the first session, about twice as many as preferable for a group of this kind. The rabbi and temple president spoke, then someone who hoped to become temple president next year spoke also. What began as a support group was becoming a replay of temple politics. There was a strong division in the group between those whose children had already intermarried and those who were interdating. The pain of these parents was palpable, and the anger and frustration were very much alive in the group; angry words were exchanged between the two subgroups. The role of the leader, especially in the early stages, should be to facilitate the group process by pointing out differences and similarities between members. Group cohesiveness was low and needed to built up over time.

Several days after the first session, the new leader received a call from the former leader and then from the rabbi. The man who would be president had contacted the old leader and asked her to return. She had consented to come out of retirement to "save" the group, and now runs several groups for this temple and others in the area.

There are many levels on which this group process, and the failure of the leader, could be analyzed. There was the politicization of the group, the important differences in gender, age, and marital status between the two group leaders, as well as their different leadership styles. But this case was chosen to illustrate two important points relating to parent groups. First, the pain and disappointment of intermarriage are usually experienced most strongly at the parental level; that is, the intermarriage is more dystonic for parents than for any other family subgroup. This intensity results in some of the clinical problems already noted, such as marital discord and family strife. In this case, the young group leader felt the brunt of many people's frustration over their children's behavior. Second, the inclusion of parents of both intermarried and interdating (or potentially interdating) children creates tensions that are not easily resolvable in the same group. For this reason, I now recommend having separate parent-support groups for these two distinct populations.

SUMMARY AND CONCLUSIONS

This article began with an overview of intermarriage as a problem for the American Jewish community in general and some American Jewish families in particular. The work of the Robert M. Beren Center was described as a psychological clinic specializing in the treatment of family-dystonic intermarriage problems prior to marriage. It was acknowledged that the clinical treatment of intermarriage-related family problems requires the clinician to consider the interface between clinical interventions and moral principles. The clinician does not work in a moral vacuum, and working with intermarriage may present particular problems for traditionally oriented Jewish clinicians and agencies. Clinicians were advised to be aware of their values and be prepared to discuss them with clients and supervisors when indicated.

A clinical approach to working with families presenting problems related to intermarriage was outlined, using family systems theory. The model includes an emphasis on system variables, such as boundaries, communication, multigenerational meanings, and family values. Clinicians must engage these families first as a consultant, then with a combination of multidirected-partiality and psychoeducational approaches, to connect with the family around questions of Jewish identity.

Families seeking help for these problems are described as struggling with family-dystonic intermarriage issues. The term "family-dystonic intermarriage" reinforces the systems perspective in both thinking about and treating these families and the individuals in them. Special considerations for parents, individuals, and couples were discussed and illustrated with case material.

The clinical problems posed by intermarriage are significant and will continue to affect the Jewish community into the twenty-first century. Parental struggles with children who interdate and intermarry, the struggles of Jewish individuals, and interfaith couples will be increasingly familiar problems that will require specialized clinical knowledge and training. This article has attempted to outline one such approach as developed at the Robert M. Beren Center at the Ferkauf Graduate School of Psychology at Yeshiva University.

This discussion would not be complete without noting one outcome of intermarriage that has received scant attention from the Jewish community: the children of intermarriage. They comprise one of the fastest-growing segments of the Jewish population, yet very little is known about their needs, attitudes, and commitments to Jewish life (Mayer 1983). A natural outgrowth of the work with interfaith couples is a commitment to help these potentially Jewish children achieve an identity that enhances their self-esteem and, where feasible, their commitment to Jewish continuity.

REFERENCES

American Psychiatric Association. 1968. *Diagnostic and Statistical Manual of Mental Disorders.* 2nd ed. Washington, D.C.: American Psychiatric Association.

————. 1987. *Diagnostic and Statistical Manual of Mental Disorders.* 3rd ed., rev. Washington, D.C.: American Psychiatric Association.

Anderson, C. M., Hogarty, G. E., and Reiss, D. J. 1980. Family treatment of adult schizophrenic patients: A psycho-educational approach. *Schizophrenia Bulletin* 6:490–505.

Aylmer, R. C. 1989. The launching of the single young adult. In *The Changing Family Life-Cycle*, ed. B. Carter and M. McGoldrick, pp. 191–208. 2nd ed. New York: Allyn & Bacon.

Boss, P., and Greenberg, J. 1984. Family boundary and ambiguity: A new variable in family stress theory. *Family Process* 23:535–546.

Boszormenyi-Nagy, I., and Spark, G. M. 1973. *Invisible Loyalties: Reciprocity in Intergenerational Family Therapy.* New York: Harper & Row.

Bowen, M. 1978. *Family Therapy in Clinical Practice.* New York: Jason Aronson.

Carter, B., and McGoldrick, M. 1989. Overview: The changing family life-cycle—a framework for family therapy. In *The Changing Family Life-Cycle*, ed. B. Carter and M. McGoldrick, pp. 3–28. 2nd ed. New York: Allyn & Bacon.

Cowan, P., and Cowan, R. 1987. *Mixed Blessings: Marriage Between Jews and Christians.* New York: Doubleday.

Crohn, J. 1986. *Ethnic Identity and Marital Conflict: Jews, Italians, and WASPs.* New York: American Jewish Committee.

Erikson, E. H. 1950. *Childhood and Society.* New York: Norton.

Fishman, S. B., Rimor, M., Tobin, G. A., and Medding, P. 1990. *Intermarriage and American Jews Today: New Findings and Policy Implications; a Summary Report.*

Waltham, Mass.: Maurice and Marilyn Cohen Center for Modern Jewish Studies, Brandeis University.

Foucault, M. 1975. *The Birth of the Clinic.* Trans. A. M. Sheridan Smith. New York: Vintage Books.

Fowler, J. W. 1981. *Stages of Faith: The Psychology of Human Development and the Quest for Meaning.* San Francisco: Harper.

Freud, S. 1923. *The Ego and the Id.* In *The Standard Edition of the Complete Psychological Works of Signmund Freud*, ed. and trans. J. Strachey, vol. 19, pp. 3–66. London: Hogarth Press, 1961.

Friedman, E. H. 1982. The myth of the shiksa. In *Ethnicity and Family Therapy*, ed. M. McGoldrick, J. K. Pearce, and J. Giordano, pp. 499–526. New York: Guilford Press.

Gordis, D. M., and Ben-Horin, Y., eds. 1991. *Jewish Identity in America.* Los Angeles: Susan and David Wilstein Institute of Jewish Policy Studies, University of Judaism.

Guerin, P. J., and Pendagast, E. G. 1976. Evaluation of family system and genogram. In *Family Therapy: Theory and Practice*, ed. P. J. Guerin, pp. 450–463. New York: Gardner Press.

Haley, J. 1967. Toward a theory of pathological systems. In *Family Therapy and Disturbed Families*, ed. G. H. Zuk and I. Boszormenyi-Nagy, pp. 11–27. Palo Alto: Science and Behavior Books.

Herz, S. M., and Rosen, E. J. 1982. Jewish families. In *Ethnicity and Family Therapy*, ed. M. McGoldrick, J. K. Pearce, and J. Giordano, pp. 364–392. New York: Guilford Press.

Hoffman, L. 1981. *Foundations of Family Therapy.* New York: Basic Books.

Kohut, H. 1977. *The Restoration of the Self.* New York: International Universities Press.

Kosmin, B. A., Goldstein, S., Waksberg, J., Lerer, N., Keysar, A., and Scheckner, J. 1991. *Highlights of the CJF 1990 National Jewish Population Survey.* New York: Council of Jewish Federations and Mandell Berman Institute—North American Jewish Data Bank, Graduate School and University Center, City University of New York.

Kosmin, B. A., Lerer, N., and Mayer, E. 1989. *Intermarriage, Divorce, and Remarriage among American Jews, 1982–1987.* New York: Mandell Berman Institute—North American Jewish Data Bank, Graduate School and University Center, City University of New York.

Linzer, N. 1984. *The Jewish Family.* New York: Human Sciences Press.

London, P. 1986. *The Modes and Morals of Psychotherapy.* 2nd ed. Washington: Hemisphere Publishing.

McCullough, P., and Rutenberg, S. 1989. Launching children and moving on. In *The Changing Family Life-Cycle*, ed. B. Carter and M. McGoldrick, pp. 285–309. 2nd ed. New York: Allyn & Bacon.

McDaniel, S. H., Weber, T. T., and Wynne, L. C. 1986. Consultants at the crossroads: Problems and controversies in systems consultation. In *Systems Consultation: A New Perspective for Family Therapy*, ed. L. C. Wynne, S. H. McDaniel, and T. T. Weber, pp. 449–462. New York: Guilford.

McGoldrick, M., and Garcia-Preto, N. 1984. Ethnic intermarriage: Implications for therapy. *Family Process* 23:347–364.

Mahler, M. S., Pine, F., and Bergman, A. 1975. *The Psychological Birth of the Human Infant: Symbiosis and Individuation.* New York: Basic Books.

Mayer, E. 1983. *Children of Intermarriage.* New York: American Jewish Committee.

———. 1985. *Love and Tradition: Marriage Between Jews and Christians.* New York: Plenum Press.

——— and Avgar, A. 1987. *Conversion Among the Intermarried: Choosing to Become Jewish.* New York: American Jewish Committee.

——— and Sheingold, C. 1979. *Intermarriage and the Jewish Future: A National Study in Summary.* New York: American Jewish Committee.

Medding, P. Y., Tobin, G. A., Fishman, S. B., and Rimor, M. 1992. Jewish identity in conversionary and mixed marriages. In *American Jewish Yearbook, 1992,* ed. D. Singer, pp. 3–76. New York: American Jewish Committee and Jewish Publication Society.

Minuchin, S. 1974. *Families and Family Therapy.* Cambridge, Mass.: Harvard University Press.

——— and Fishman, H. C. 1981. *Family Therapy Techniques.* Cambridge, Mass.: Harvard University Press.

Packouz, K. 1976. *How to Stop an Intermarriage.* Jerusalem: Intermarriage Crises Conference.

Paul, G. D. 1993. Intermarriage in USA reaches 57 per cent. *Jewish Chronicle,* Jan. 22, p. 8.

Perel, E. 1990. Ethnocultural factors in marital communication among intermarried couples. *Journal of Jewish Communal Service* 66:28–37.

Petsonk, J. 1990. Sensitizing Jewish professionals to intermarriage issues in counseling, group work, and education. *Journal of Jewish Communal Service* 66:254–269.

——— and Remsen, J. 1988. *The Intermarriage Handbook.* New York: Quill.

Phinney, J. S. 1990. Ethnic identity in adolescents and adults: Review of research. *Psychological Bulletin* 108:499–514.

Reiss, D. 1981. *The Family's Construction of Reality.* Cambridge, Mass.: Harvard University Press.

Satir, V. 1964. *Conjoint Family Therapy: A Guide to Theory and Technique.* Palo Alto: Science and Behavior Books.

Schneider, S. W. 1989. *Intermarriage: The Challenge of Living with Differences Between Christians and Jews.* New York: Free Press.

Simon, F. B., Stierlin, H., and Wynne, L. C. 1985. *The Language of Family Therapy: A Systemic Vocabulary and Sourcebook.* New York: Family Process Press.

Sirkin, M. I. 1990. Cult involvement: A systems approach to assessment and treatment. *Psychotherapy* 27:116–123.

———. 1992. The abiding alien: Representations of Jewish alienation in science fiction. Unpublished manuscript.

———. 1993. Responding to intermarriage: Effective rabbinic intervention. *Rabbinics Today,* pp. 1–3. March.

——— and Grellong, B. A. 1988. Cult vs. non-cult Jewish families: Factors influencing conversion. *Cultic Studies Journal* 5:2–21.

——— and Rueveni, U. 1992. The role of network therapy in the treatment of relational disorder: Cults and folie a deux. *Contemporary Family Therapy* 14:211–224.

——— and Wynne, L. C. 1990. Cult involvement as a relational disorder.

Psychiatric Annals 20:199–203.

Speck, R. V., and Attneave, C. L. 1973. *Family Networks.* New York: Pantheon Books.

Spickard, P. R. 1989. *Mixed Blood: Intermarriage and Ethnic Identity in Twentieth Century America.* Madison: University of Wisconsin Press.

Szasz, T. S. 1970. *The Manufacture of Madness.* New York: Harper.

Vogel, E. F., and Bell, N. W. 1960. The emotionally disturbed child as the family scapegoat. In *The Family,* ed. E. F. Vogel and N. W. Bell, pp. 412–427. Glencoe, Ill.: Free Press.

Watzlawick, P., Weakland, J. W., and Fisch, R. 1974. *Change: Principles of Problem Formation and Problem Resolution.* New York: Norton.

NOTES

1. The family therapy literature abounds with terms that connote hypo-individuation or a lack of autonomy (Simon, Stierlin, and Wynne 1985). The terms "autonomy" and "interconnectedness," when used together, connote an ideal for families and individuals.

2. The term "dystonic," the complement of "syntonic," was adapted from medicine by ego psychologists and incorporated into DSM-II (American Psychiatric Association 1968). Certain psychiatric problems, such as antisocial behavior and homosexuality, were said to be ego-syntonic when they did not create discomfort for the person, but created discomfort for others or were illegal. Ego-dystonic problems were those which did create discomfort, guilt, etc. In current, DSM-III-R jargon (American Psychiatric Association 1989), Axis II personality disorders are considered ego-syntonic.

JEWISH FAMILY:
MID-LIFE AND BEYOND

Michael J. Salamon

Jews share a common historical, religious, cultural, ethnic, and even social heritage, but there is a broad degree of variation among different groups of Jews. This heterogeneity can take a variety of forms, ranging from subtle distinctions in communal affiliations to widely discrepant philosophies of what constitutes true Jewish family life. Three areas where the broadest range of variance can be found among older Jews in the United States is in degree of acculturation, religiosity, and occupation.

IMMIGRANT BACKGROUND AND ACCULTURATION

Family relationships change in adapting to a new society, but families of different cultural backgrounds do not become the same (Woehrer 1982). So too the Jewish family retains its mutuality but is also affected by ethnic tradition, country of origin, and degree of acculturation.

Immigration to the United States took place in waves, almost always following a pogrom or similar tragedy and culminating in the largest Jewish emigration from Europe following the Holocaust. Adjusting to the new life in America was dependent upon several factors. Those who came from the urban centers of Europe adjusted to life in the United States at a more rapid pace than Jews who were from small shtetls or Middle Eastern countries. Jews tended to settle in small communities with others of similar background, maintaining many of the Old World family traditions, language, even trades (Meyerhoff and Simic 1978).

Elders within the Jewish communities of America attempted to transmit traditional values as they understood them. To their children modern lifestyles only confirmed the lessening value of old ways. The tension created in these situations was heightened by the fact that many older family members came to America without their own parents and grandparents. The guilt of the Holocaust survivors and the sense of having abandoned family members in other situations may never have been resolved (Salamon, in press). For many this tension caused the exertion of additional pressure in an attempt to keep the Jewish family functioning as it did in the old country, shielding the modern family from the new culture.

Adaptation and acculturation to America took place within the greater American community at a more rapid pace than within the home. In spite of prejudice and ostracism Jews managed, through educational achievement, to go on to the highest levels of success in the professions (Auerbach 1976; Howe 1976). What is striking is the discrepancy between the older generation's resources and their own children's success. Most Jewish immigrants arrived in America penniless. Their children went on to become professionals. Eighty-two percent of the adult children of Holocaust survivors, for example, have been found to have become professionals (Kahane and Kahane 1984). The message given to children in the family was a powerful one that stressed the need for achievement.

It has been argued that Jewish women immigrants have followed the traditional sex roles of total devotion to family and socialization of children (Jacoby 1979), while the second-generation immigrant daughter is growing up with more modern, liberated sex roles. The implication is that younger Jewish women will transcend the limited success of their mothers. This may be true in terms of professional success, and it is a known fact that more married Jewish women are gainfully employed in nonprofessional positions than women of any other ethnic group (Krause 1978). Of those adult women who report being Jewish, 53 percent are employed (Kosmin 1991).

The trend toward acculturation outside the home was further balanced by the Jewish concept of tzedakah. More than charity, tzedakah refers to the concept of communal responsibility for those in need. While many individuals view financial contributions as the easiest way to discharge responsibility to the Jewish community, the concept of greater family responsibility is especially strong among Jews. It has been reported that in 1992 the most successful charity in the United States was UJA Federation (*New York Times*, Jan. 12, 1993, p. B3).

The Jewish family, in spite of its outward acculturation, appears to retain a strong sense of heritage within its confines. This, to a degree, is strengthened by the immigrant background of family elders (Knight 1986) but also by charity and a conceptualization of the unique sense of Jewishness transmitted across the generations. In the United States, there are growing signs of movement away from this uniqueness.

RELIGION

Religious affiliation and degree of religious devotion are individual decisions that have been highly related to overall well-being and adjustment to aging (Salamom 1979; Stambler 1982). In the United States today approximately 10–12 percent of Jews are reported to be Orthodox, 40 percent Conservative, and 35 percent Reform. The remaining 15 percent of Jews are reported to be unaffiliated (Kosmin et al. 1991). Since 1900 Jews have become less religiously involved with each succeeding generation, while most other religious groups in America have shown an increase in religious affiliation over the same time period (Lachman and Kosmin 1990). Older and foreign-born Jews are found to be among the more religiously devoted. It has also been reported that as Jewish men age they attend religious services more frequently (Orbach 1961). However, proportionally more Catholics attend religious services more frequently than Jews in every age group (Wingrove and Alston 1971, 1974), and more than 60 percent of American Jews spend only three days or less a year at religious services (Lachman and Kosmin 1990).

Several studies of adjustment to the aging process indicate that Jews who were more religious in their beliefs tended to adjust better than nonobservant coreligionists. Thirty-three Jewish women between the ages of sixty-five and eighty-three were interviewed regarding their adaptation to physical aging (Siegel 1976). It was found that religion provides for a compensatory scheme of adaptation to physical losses experienced with increasing age (Markides 1983). Similarly, a group of fifteen elderly Jewish men who attended regular study sessions were followed and matched with male coreligionists who did not attend these groups. Those involved in education were less depressed and reported higher levels of life satisfaction (Salamon 1979). Orthodox Jews were also found to have more positive overall adjustment to the aging process (Moberg 1968). Further, it has been found that religious faith strengthens the individual's ability to deal with grief and bereavement (Heller 1975: Woods and Britton 1985).

Religious devotion in America appears to be on the wane among younger Jews (Lachman and Kosmin 1990). This is of particular concern because it threatens Jewish identity. As Jewish identity fades, the unique contribution of the Jewish religion begins to disappear.

OCCUPATION

Work is seen among Jewish family members as the force leading to betterment of the individual and society. As Jews have become more rooted in American society, occupational growth and success have grown significantly. The National Jewish Population Survey found that 50 percent of Jews in their early sixties were upper-level managers or administrators. Approximately 18 percent were technical or professional workers, and about 5 percent were employed in sales. Of those aged sixty-five to seventy-five,

35 percent had been in management and 20 percent were professional or technical workers. The majority of females who reported working had been employed in clerical positions.

What is significant is the increasing move toward professional careers across the decades. Academically, 70 percent of those 65 or older did not go on to higher education beyond high school. Of those aged fifty to sixty-four, only 50 percent did not go beyond high school, while 50 percent attained a college degree or higher.

Over the past several years there has been some concern that retirement is a precipitant for mental illness, especially depression, in old age. There are several studies which indicate that older Jews, as a group, tend to volunteer more than other ethnic groups, at about 40 percent, and formal social participation is extensive among older Jews (Kahane and Kahane 1984).

The impact of older Jews' involvement in leisure activities and volunteerism on younger family members would at first appear to be beneficial. It is good that everyone has something productive to do (Sandler 1992). It fosters a sense of ongoing independence and accomplishment. On the other hand, should older individuals become frail or unable to continue on with their independent lifestyle, the family's adjustment difficulties become more pronounced and occur at a more rapid pace. This change can cause heightened family tensions unique to families striving over the course of lifetimes for success.

In spite of the broad variations found among Jewish families, Jews share a cultural style characterized by their background, religion, and striving for occupational success (Katz 1975). This unifying theme is becoming increasingly tenuous in the United States as a result of the threats to Jewish family life.

JEWISH FAMILY

For older adults, family relationships are the number-one priority ahead of all other social interactions (Guttmann 1979). As children grow up they are socialized to specific formats of interaction. Young Jewish children are given emotional support, encouragement, and praise. As adults they in turn visit their parents more frequently than adult children of other ethnic groups (Greeley 1971). Reciprocity coupled with the closeness of the family serves to explain the intensity of Jewish family life.

Structure of Support

Role structure within a family is generally determined by the degree of authority, cultural ideals regarding relationships, and how responsibility is distributed. Jewish families tend to be patriarchal in fewer ways than other ethnic groups. The father has the majority responsibility for financial support of the family, but in the most traditional of Jewish families this responsibility may be abrogated in part for the furtherance of religion. Jewish mothers have contributed to the family in many ways, including sharing financial responsibility and most child-rearing. Thus, Jewish wives command equal respect to that of their husbands.

While there have recently been many studies of the sense of responsibility between aged spouses (Blieszner and Hamon 1992), the sense of intergenerational responsibility and degree of support between generations within the family have not been well documented. Further, there is ambiguity in the results that have been reported, and there have been no significant studies of specific ethnic trends.

Several studies of filial responsibility, the sense of responsibility to assist and support the well-being of older family members (Blieszner and Hamon 1992), are of value in understanding the Jewish family. In an early study of attitudes toward family support, 1,006 college and 318 high school students were surveyed. The results of this study indicated that Catholics and residents of rural areas endorsed the responsibility of support toward older family members more than Protestants, Jews, and those not religiously affiliated (Dinkel 1944). In a replication of the study done thirty years later (Wake and Sporakowski 1972), 119 college and 136 high school students were interviewed. In this study no significant difference was found in sense of filial responsibility between rural or urban residents or religious denominations. The only finding of significance in this study was that the youngest female sibling reported the greatest intensity of filial responsibility. Similar results of no difference were found more recently (Finley, Roberts, and Banahan 1988). In this latter study, however, the authors concluded that filial responsibility is a result of the respondent's life circumstances, in particular, the degree of affection daughters feel toward their fathers, mothers, and mothers-in-law, rather than religion or birth order. Perhaps the earlier findings were an artifact of the large sample size.

Overall, the motivation for filial support tends to result from a sense of obligation and moral imperative (Walker et al. 1989). Jewish tradition emphasizes the importance of care for elders as a means of helping to allay fears of abandonment. This is especially noted in terms of intergenerational family support (Smolar 1985). In an early study of Jewish families, Bressler (1952) reviewed family correspondence and found that Jews had a strong sense of obligation toward their family members. Similarly, a small study of college students found that Jewish students appeared to have higher rates of happy relationships with their parents than did their Catholic and Protestant peers (Landis 1960). Bordis (1961), however, found that devotion to the family was no higher for Jewish respondents than Protestants. While there is no apparent pattern of support unique to Jewish families, our present small-scale studies suggest that the sense of family commitment remains strong across the generations. Some have suggested that this is due to the unique ideal of Jewish survival (Holzberg 1982).

SURVIVORS

When one speaks of survivors and Jews the focus turns immediately to the Holocaust. Survivors suffer from what has been referred to as "never ending mourning" (Fried and Waxman 1988). They have, and continue to show, signs of rage, guilt, masochistic behavior, psychosomatic disease, and anxiety. They may be socially withdrawn and less emotionally stable, with continuing difficulty forming close emotional attachments (Nadler and Ben-Shushan 1989). While these symptoms are exacerbated by individual characterological deficits (Salamon, in press), the impact on the family emerges even in those families where survivors display few or no symptoms (Epstein 1979).

One of the better-documented reactions appears to be that children of survivors are less likely to externalize aggression (Nadler, Kav-Venaki, and Gleitman 1985), reverting to guilt as a motivator. Children of survivors are viewed by their parents as the source of hope and meaning in their lives. This may create a burden of expectation on the child that is unrealistic. The child in turn feels an obligation to exhibit an extreme degree of consideration for the parents (Philips 1978). This method of interaction is manipulative and based on internalized guilt.

Survivorship as a philosophical approach to life for Jews, however, is not limited to those who survived the Holocaust. Having suffered persecution or discrimination, Jews view survival as a cultural imperative. In spite of having put aside a good deal of their Judaic heritage earlier in their lives, older Jews strongly adhere to the survival of Jewish culture (Meyerhoff 1978). Some research noted above suggests a positive relationship between age and regular religious service attendance for Jewish men. In addition, overall devotion to the symbols of Jewish family heritage increases significantly with age. Thus family holiday celebrations, such as the Passover Seder and High Holiday family get-togethers, become a source for the Jewish family, even the unaffiliated, with which to maintain a semblance of continuing Jewish identity. One can see strong examples of this in Jewish-sponsored senior centers.

RECIPROCITY

For the Jewish family to survive there is a need for a social balance in the relationship between the generations. Social support between the generations has been documented to have beneficial outcome for a variety of physical and psychological ailments (Antonucci and Jackson 1990). It is also related to the individual's ability to cope with life and the aging process (Rowe and Kahn 1987).

The concept of reciprocity, that partners to a relationship achieve a balance in what they offer each other, is important in understanding family interaction (Salamon 1986). Long-term intimate relationships are based on an assumption of reciprocity over many years. For example, parents provide for children early in life as an investment for their own needs as they age. This is not a financial consideration; rather, it is a complex psychological issue influenced by individual variability, sociodemographic factors, and other external variables.

Three theories have been used to explain reciprocity between the generations. Equity theory indicates that reciprocity is based upon a desire to maintain homeostasis, or a complete balance, in relationships (Brody 1985). Just as homeostasis is unconscious for biological mechanisms, so too for social ones. The second theory is based upon the conscious sense of obligation. While it is similar to equity, it requires more of a conscious effort to feel the obligation of maintaining a balance in the relationship (Cicirelli 1989). Attachment is the third explanation for reciprocity. This theoretical position suggests that balance is maintained solely as a reaction to the intensity of the affectional bond (Wynne 1991).

Reciprocity has been studied in a variety of groups. Blacks over the age of eighteen reported increased happiness in relationships when there was clear reciprocity (Antonucci and Jackson 1990; Clark and Reis 1988). Further, those who report receiving more than they gave were significantly happier than those receiving less than they gave in a social/family relationship. Among disabled adults, blacks tended to report happiness if the relationship was balanced or if they received more than they gave. However, white respondents who were disabled tended to report lower levels of happiness when the exchange was reciprocal or when they were receiving more than they gave.

The degree of reciprocity in Jewish families appears to be higher than among other ethnic groups. This relates to the earlier premise that Jewish families have a greater degree of intensity than others, given their identification as survivors (Landis 1960; Sanua 1974). This intensity of kinship is evidenced by the degree of contact Jewish family members report with members of their extended families. For example, in a study of residents of an Arizona retirement community (Farber 1981), Jews reported more contact with family members than any other religious group. Catholics reported frequent contact with mothers-in-law only 35 percent of the time, while Jews reported it 65 percent of the time. Ninety percent of the Jews surveyed reported contact with older parents at least once a week, as opposed to 50 percent among other groups. And Jews reported higher degrees of contact with grandparents than the other religious groups surveyed (Greeley 1971).

When the intensity of reciprocal relationships is applied to studies of ethnic groups, it has been found that older Polish family members report feeling abandoned by their families more frequently than other groups. Jewish, Italian, and Slavic women have a greater degree of intensity than other groups in terms of their ability to interact on an emotional level, sharing feelings and responding to reciprocal needs (Krause 1979).

Intensely reciprocal relationships may become unbalanced. While Jewish families appear to be willing to accept the burden of caring for their older family members more frequently than some other religious or ethnic groups, problems may occur if adult Jewish children feel their parents are too emotionally dependent on them (Simos 1973). Even when strong support networks with well-balanced degrees of exchange exist, families turn to larger cultural and social networks for assistance.

SERVICE UTILIZATION

Jewish families are noted for their charitable tradition. However, especially for the oldest generation, the desire to help others does not always extend to oneself. In studies performed in Los Angeles, Chicago, and New York, it has been found that those most at risk and with the highest degree of need in the Jewish community are the least likely to use available social services (Huberman 1984, 1986).

It has been suggested that asking for help is a difficult task for adults and older adults (Cantor 1989; Salamon 1981; Woods and Britton 1985), but this is apparently much more the case among Jewish families. Approximately 15 percent of Jewish New Yorkers are at or below the poverty level, about half of whom are over the age of sixty-five. Nevertheless, over 60 percent report no direct contact with social service agencies. This is likely the result of a stigma attached to seeking aid from others, significantly more pronounced when the aid is related to coping with mental illness.

MENTAL HEALTH NEEDS

Jews have the same mental illnesses, psychoses, neuroses, and psychopathologies as other ethnic groups. Research over the years, however, indicates that there are some qualitative differences in rates of prevalence and incidence (Sanua 1979, 1981). Overall Jews appear to have low rates of psychosis, schizophrenia, alcoholism, other addictions, and psychoses of organic origin. They do have high rates for neuroses and bipolar disorders, the latter possibly linked to genetics (Horgan 1993). It has also been suggested that Jews have an historically legitimate reason for hypervigilance.

Jewish women tend to suffer clinical depression more than either black or non-Jewish white women, explained as a by-product of the strong maternal emotional tie in the Jewish family. When the maternal role is lost, empty nest (cf. Harris 1988) is more severe an adjustment for Jewish mothers. There is also a higher rate of eating disorders and a lower rate of suicide among Jews. Where there are cases of addictive disorder or social deviance, more significant psychopathology tends be the underlying factor.

What these studies suggest is that strong family bonds reduce the likelihood of addiction and suicide in Jewish families.

Help-seeking Behaviors

In instances where neuroses exist, Jews tend to be more goal-oriented. In seeking treatment they do not look for symptom removal, rather they seek a complete cure. This behavior also exists for physical illness. There is some indication that Jews tend to attempt self-care for their physical pain more frequently than other ethnic groups, at least during the early stages of illness. They turn to their family for help with minor issues related to compensating for physical pain and help in overcoming mild acute ailments. Irish-Americans, when ill, prefer to be alone and do not generally complain. Jewish- and Italian-Americans do not withdraw from their families, because suffering is seen as part of the living process (Woehrer 1982). This is consistent with the reciprocity found in Jewish families.

Individuals over the age of sixty-five use the wide range of health care services available to them at a much higher rate than younger people (Binstock 1985). Some researchers have found that Jewish patients are more likely than others to make use of medical facilities and report more symptoms than other groups (Kahane and Kahane 1984). While it is difficult to confirm this finding in large-scale studies, research performed at the Adult

Developmental Center suggests that it is likely the case. In our observations we have found that attendance at senior centers increases dramatically on the days that a medical service, such as blood pressure screening, is offered.

What we find, then, is that Jews will first bring their ailments to the attention of their family members. When that support is no longer sufficient, they turn to professional health care providers more rapidly and with more detail than individuals of other ethnic groups. They are more likely to turn to medical support, however, than to any other organized support.

FAMILY SUPPORT NETWORKS

Much has been made of the dissolution of the modern family. Emphasis has been placed on the decline of the extended family. Research, however, has shown that the three-generation family all living under one roof was never the norm in the United States (Hagestad 1985). When intergenerational families do live together, it is because one of the generations does not have the financial means to live alone, health of a family member is poor, self-care is tenuous, or the adult child is unmarried (Troll 1982).

While the generations tend not to live together, researchers have found that the two oldest generations in the family tend to live near one another. Seventy-five percent of older adults who live alone report a child living within 30 minutes travel time, and 80 percent report a child living within less than an hour's travel time (Hagestad 1985; Troll 1982). Support that is offered between the generations is less likely to be financial and more likely to be emotional or service-oriented. Thus, families will help identify the needs of their older family members so that the appropriate institutions can address them (Salamon and Rosenthal 1990).

Jewish tradition requires unconditional respect for elders, but the mandate for care is more option-based. Filial obligation, however, is altered when the parent suffers from a dementia. The child is responsible for arranging care for the parent but not for providing direct care on their own (Meier 1977).

SENIOR AND COMMUNITY CENTERS

In the late 1960s and early 1970s federal funding was made available for the establishment of senior centers, to offer recreation, socialization, and nutrition programs for those not properly cared for in the community. In New York City many senior centers were opened under the auspices of Jewish communal organizations and synagogue groups.

Older individuals have, over the years, received services from these senior centers; however, federally funded programs appear not to have met their original goals. Problems with centers for older adults include overemphasis on meals, so that individuals will attend at lunchtime only and not make use of other available services; inadequate sensitivity to the unique quality of the local community being serviced; rules promulgated that are not sensitive to local traditions; and a lack of older-adult investment in programs (Salamon 1981). These problems appear to affect Jewish attendees at senior centers in a significant fashion. In her detailed study of one center in California, Meyerhoff (1978) observed that many of the members of the center were tightly bound to one another but their relationships never coalesced into those usually observed in many other social organizations. Daily center life was described as dramatic and tumultuous, fraught with tension and contradiction. Recent observations performed at senior centers indicate that not much has changed.

Older Jews do not appear to make a firm bond to senior centers because of the three problems just cited. Individuals attend for lunch only as a convenience and view the program itself as charity-based, though center members are asked to volunteer with programming and to contribute a voluntary fee. Furthermore, center life does not always reflect their own ideological and traditional desires for social interactions.

In contrast to senior centers, community centers appear to be more widely used by older adults (General Accounting Office 1977). In a survey performed by the Jewish Community Forum of Cleveland, Jewish respondents reported greater use of the Jewish Community Center and Jewish-sponsored community programs than other available services. Perhaps they tend to partake of these programs because they are directly sponsored by Jewish organizations and display a strong identification with Jewish culture and heritage.

INSTITUTIONALIZATION

Popular opinion as well as individual guilt have motivated individuals to believe that frail older adults receive better care at home than in an institution. Research has shown that such is not always the case (Salamon 1987).

Recent trends regarding institutional care of the aged have emphasized care for the more medically frail. For example, in the United States today there are over 120 nonprofit institutions under Jewish sponsorship providing services for the ill older adult. The majority of these are filled to capacity and have long waiting lists for admission. Still, there are many reasons why the frail elderly cannot be cared for at home. There are few care providers available, and the services that exist tend to be informal and provided by relatives with limited physical, emotional, and financial resources. Further, the needs of older family members may be extreme and the facilities at home inadequate (Salamon and Rosenthal 1990). We have also found that because of the low fertility rate among Jews, there are fewer middle-aged children among Jews than among other ethnic groups to provide care at home.

Given these limited resources, Jewish families are placing their frail elderly in facilities not under Jewish auspices. When this occurs there are three factors that appear to impact on the decision: (a) availability of religious services, (b) kosher meals, and (c) location that allows for easier family visitation (Salamon 1988). When these three factors are available in a non-Jewish setting, family members are more likely to feel sufficiently comfortable with the facility to place their frail relative.

FUTURE TRENDS

As we have seen, it is difficult to obtain specific data on Jewish families in the United States. What we are finding is that Jewish couples are divorcing at rates at least equivalent to the population at large (Gelfand and Olsen 1979; Lachman and Kosmin 1990). At the same time, intermarriage rates for younger Jews are increasing dramatically (Kosmin et al. 1991). Reports indicate that many Reform synagogues have memberships that can be as high as 50 percent not Jewish (Lachman and Kosmin 1990). Non-Jews seek membership by virtue of marriage to a Jewish individual. Further, the fertility rate for Jewish families is perhaps the lowest of all religions, not only in America but in Israel as well.

In addition to these trends, Jewish families in the United States tend to be among the most successful, yet Jewish older adults are among the largest numbers reporting high rates of poverty. Increasing involvement in professional careers and financial success has been linked with decreasing family and religious involvement (Kahane and Kahane 1984).

All of these trends bode ill for the Jewish family. When there are fewer Jewish children within a Jewish family that is less affiliated and more likely to condone intermarriage (Haberman 1992), religious identity is weakened. As we have seen, when cultural and historical ties are broken, Jewish families lose their unique status. Jews already have proportionally fewer families with children and more people living alone than any other ethnic or religious group in the United States (Lachman and Kosmin 1990). Yet while professional commitments may mean that they do not have the time to care for their elders, and there are too few children to share the burden, they do support institutions that can provide care.

In contrast, there appears to be a trend toward increasing interest in Jewish tradition and observance among middle-aged and younger Jews. This trend is most obvious among groups such as NCSY and CJY, organizations designed to attract unaffiliated teenagers and young adults. While involvement in one of these organizations does not necessarily increase religious observance, unaffiliated individuals display a resurgence of pride in their Judaism. Similarly, Jewish community organizations and institutions are also displaying and advocating stronger adherence to religious precepts. Still, American Jews are moving away from traditional forms of Judaism.

Research designed to investigate this issue is sorely lacking. Some Jewish outreach programs exist but they are insufficient, and dwindling affiliation, if not reversed, could create a serious threat to the Jewish family and to Jewish elders in particular. If middle-aged Jews do not set the example for their own care by providing for their parents, who will be left to care for them?

REFERENCES

Antonucci, T. C., and Jackson, J. S. 1990. The role of reciprocity in social support. In *Social Support: An Interactional View*, ed. B. R. Sarason, I. G. Sarason, and G. R. Pierce. New York, Wiley.

Auerbach, J. S. 1976. From rags to robes: The legal profession, social mobility and the American Jewish experience. *American Jewish Historical Quarterly* 65:249–284.

Bardis, P. D. 1961. Familism among Jews in suburbia. *Social Science* 36:190–196.

Binstock, R. H. 1985. Heath care of the aging: Trends, dilemmas and prospects of the year 2000. In *Aging 2000: Our Health Care Destiny*, ed. C. M. Gaitz, G. Niederehe, and N. L. Wilson. New York. Springer-Verlag.

Bressler, M. 1952. Selected family patterns. *American Sociological Review* 17:563–571.

Blieszner, R., and Hamon, R. R. 1992. Filial responsibility: Attitudes, motivators and behaviors. In *Gender, Families and Elder Care*, ed. J. W. Dwyer and R. T. Coward. Newbury Park, Calif.: Sage.

Brody, E. M. 1985. Parent care as a normative family stress. *Gerontologist* 25:19–29.

Cantor, M. M. Social care: Family and community support systems. *Annals of the American Academy of Political and Social Science* 503:99–112.

Cicirelli, V. G. 1989. Helping relationships in later life: A reexamination. In *Aging Parents and Adult Children*, ed. J. A. Mancini. Lexington, Mass.: Lexington Books.

Clark, M. S., and Reis, H. T. 1988. Interpersonal processes in close relationships. In *Annual Review of Psychology* 39:609–612.

Council of Jewish Federations. 1973. *The Jewish Aging: Facts for Planning*. New York: Council of Jewish Federations.

Dinkel, R. 1944. Attitudes of children toward supporting aged parents. *American Sociological Review* 9:370–379.

Epstein, H. 1979. *Children of the Holocaust: Conversations with Sons and Daughters of Survivors*. New York: Putnam.

Farber, B. 1981. *Conceptions of Kinship*. New York. Elsevier.

Finley, N. J., Roberts, M. D., and Banahan, B. F. 1988. Motivators and inhibitors of attitudes of filial obligation toward aging parents. *Gerontologist* 28:73–78.

Fried, H., and Waxman, H. M. 1988. Stockholm's Cafe 84: A unique day program for Jewish survivors of concentration camps. *Gerontologist* 25:253–255.

Gelfand, D. E., and Olsen, J. 1979. Aging in the Jewish family and the Mormon family. In *Ethnicity and Aging: Theory, Research and Policy*, ed. D. E. Gelfand and A. Kutzik. New York, Springer.

General Accounting Office. 1977. The well-being of older people in Cleveland, Ohio. Washington, D.C.: U.S. Government Printing Office.

Goldstein, S. 1982. Population movement and redistribution among American Jews. *Jewish Journal of Sociology* 14:4–23.

Gortler, J. 1979. *A Study of the Jewish Community in the Greater Seattle Area*, Seattle: Jewish Community Federation of Seattle.

Greeley, A. M. 1971. *Why Can't They Be Like Us?* New York: Dutton.

Greeley, M. 1974. *Ethnicity in the United States: A Preliminary Reconnaissance.* New York: Wiley.

Guttman, D. 1979. Use of informal and formal supports by white ethnic aged. In *Ethnicity and Aging: Theory Research and Policy*, ed. D. E. Gelfand and A. J. Kutzick. New York: Springer.

Haberman, C. 1992. Israel study finds birthrate at lowest since 1948. *New York Times*, Nov. 7, p. A12.

Hagestad, G. O. 1985. Vertical bonds. In *The Adult Years: Continuity and Change*, ed. G. O. Schlossberg. Owings Mills, Md.: International University Consortium.

Harris, D. K. 1988. *Dictionary of Gerontology*, Westport, Conn.: Greenwood Press.

Heller, Z. I. 1975. The Jewish view of death: Guidelines for dying. In *Death: The Final Stage of Growth*, ed. E. Kubler-Ross. Englewood Cliffs, N.J.: Prentice-Hall.

Holzberg, C. S. 1982. Ethnicity and aging: Anthropological perspectives on more than just the minority elderly. *Gerontologist* 22:249–257.

Horgan, J. 1993. Eugenics revisited. *Scientific American* 268, no. 6:122–131.

Howe, I. 1976. *World of Our Fathers.* New York: Harcourt Brace Jovanovich.

Huberman, S. 1984. Growing old in Jewish America: A study of Jewish aged in Los Angeles. *Journal of Jewish Communal Service* 60:314–323.

———. 1986. Jews in economic distress. *Journal of Jewish Communal Service* 62:197–208.

Jacoby, S. 1979. World of our mothers: Immigrant women, immigrant daughters. *Present Tense* 6:48–51.

Kahane E., and Kahane, B. 1984. Jews. In *Handbook on the Aged in the United States*, ed. E. B. Palmore. Westport, Conn.: Greenwood Press.

Katz, R. L. 1975. Jewish values and sociopsychological perspectives on aging. *Pastoral Psychology* 24:135–150.

Knight, B. 1986. *Psychotherapy with Older Adults*. Naubary Park, Calif.: Sage.

Kosmin, B. A., Goldstein, S., Waksberg, J., Lerer, N., Keysar, A., and Schecker, J. 1991. *Highlights of the CJF 1990 National Jewish Population Survey.* New York: Council of Jewish Federations.

Krause, C. A. 1978. *Grandmothers, Mothers, Daughters.* New York: American Jewish Committee.

Lachman, S. P., and Kosmin, B. A. 1990. What is happening to American Jewry? *New York Times*, June 4.

Landis, J. T. 1960. Religiousness, family religion and family value in Protestant, Catholic and Jewish families. *Marriage and Family Living* 22:341–347.

Markides, K. S. 1983. Aging, religiosity and adjustment: A longitudinal analysis. *Journal of Gerontology* 38:621–625.

Massarik, F., and Chenkin, A. 1973. United States' National Jewish Population Study. *American Jewish Yearbook*, vol. 74. Philadelphia: Jewish Publication Society.

Meier, L. 1977. Filial responsibility to the senile parent: A Jewish approach. *Journal of Psychology and Judaism* 2:45–53.

Meyerhoff, B. 1978. *Number Our Days*. New York: Touchstone.

——— and Simic, A. 1978. *Life's Career—Aging: Cultural Variations in Growing Old*. Beverly Hills, Calif.: Sage.

Moberg, D. O. 1968. Religiosity in old age. In *Middle Age and Aging*, ed. B. Neugarten. Chicago: University of Chicago Press.

Nadler, A., and Ben-Shushan. 1989. Forty years later: Long-term consequences of massive traumatization as manifested by Holocaust survivors from the city and the kibbutz. *Journal of Consulting and Clinical Psychology* 57:287–293.

————, Kav Venaki, S., and Gleitman, B. 1985. Transgenerational effects of the Holocaust: Externalization of aggression in second generation of Holocaust survivors. *Journal of Consulting and Clinical Psychology* 53:365–369.

Orbach, H. L. 1961. Aging and religion: Church attendance in the Detroit metropolitan area. *Geriatrics* 11:356–358.

Philips, R. E. 1978. Impact of the Nazi Holocaust on the children of survivors. *American Journal of Psychotherapy* 32:370–378.

Prager, E. H. 1986. Elderly movers to Israel. *Journal of Cross-Cultural Gerontology* 1:91–102.

Rosenwaike, I. 1974. Estimating Jewish population distribution in U.S. metropolitan areas in 1970. *Jewish Social Studies* 36:106–117.

————. 1986. The American Jewish elderly in transition. *Journal of Jewish Communal Service* 62:283–291.

————. 1991–92. Estimating the geographic distribution of America's Jewish elderly: A surname analysis. *Journal of Jewish Communal Service* 68:160–168.

Rowe, J., and Kahn, R. L. 1987. Human aging: Usual and successful. *Science* 237:143–149.

Salamon, M. J. 1979. Limud-Torah: A fountain of youth. *Jewish Press* 29, no. 6, p. 15.

————. 1981. Senior centers: Are they really for seniors? *New England Journal of Human Services* 4:26–30.

————. 1986. *A Basic Guide to Working with Elders.* New York: Springer.

————. 1987. Health care environment and life satisfaction in the aged. *Journal of Aging Studies* 1:79–88.

————. 1988. Jewish patients in nursing homes under non-Jewish auspices: Some personal observations. *Journal of Aging and Judaism* 2:196–200.

————. in press. Coping and defense mechanisms of survivors: Denial and acceptance. *Clinical Gerontologist.*

———— and Rosenthal, G. 1990. *Home or Nursing Home: Making the Right Choice.* New York: Springer.

Sandler, R. 1992. *Senior Pursuits*, Miami, Fla.: Valiant Press.

Sanua, V. D. 1974. The contemporary Jewish family. *Journal of Jewish Communal Service* 50:297–312.

———. 1979. Psychopathology among Jews. Paper presented at Convention of American Psychological Association, New York.

———. 1981. Psychopathology and social deviance among Jews. *Journal of Jewish Communal Service* 58:11–17.

Siegel, M. K. 1976. A Jewish aging experience: A description of the role of religion in response to physical dysfunction in a sample of Jewish women. Doctoral diss., Harvard University. *Dissertation Abstracts International* 38 (2A), 722.

Simos, B. 1973. Adult children and their aging parents. *Social Work* 18:75–85.

Smolar, L. 1985. Context and text: Realities and Jewish perspectives on the aged. *Journal of Jewish Communal Service* 62:1–7.

Stambler, M. 1982. Jewish ethnicity and aging. *Journal of Jewish Communal Service* 58:336–342.

Troll, L. E. 1982. Family life in middle and old age: The generation gap. *Annals of the American Academy of Political and Social Science* 464:38–46.

Wake, S. B., and Sporakowski, M. J. 1972. An intergenerational comparison of attitudes toward supporting aged parents. *Journal of Marriage and the Family* 34:42–48.

Walker, A. J., Pratt, C. C., Shin, H. Y., and Jones, L. L. 1989. Why daughters care: Perspectives of mothers and daughters in caregiving situations. In *Aging Parents and Adult Children*, ed. J. A. Mancini. Lexington, Mass.: Lexington Books.

Wingrove, C. R., and Alston, J. 1971. Age, aging and church attendance. *Gerontologist* 11:356–358.

——— and Alston, J. 1974. Cohort analysis of church attendance, 1939–1969. *Social Forces* 53:324–331.

Woehrer, C. E. 1982. The influence of ethnic families on inter-generational relationships and later life transitions. *Annals of the American Academy of Political and Social Science* 464:65–78.

Woods, R. T., and Britton, P. G. 1985. *Clinical Psychology with the Elderly.* Rockville, Md.: Aspen.

Wynne, E. A. 1991. Will the young support the old? In *Growing Old in America*, ed. B. B. Hess and E. W. Markson. 4th ed. New Brunswick, N.J.: Transaction Publishers.

CARING FOR THE INCAPACITATED PARENT: FILIAL OBLIGATION IN CLASSIC JEWISH SOURCES

David J. Schnall

I.

Recent analyses of the Jewish family and its contemporary concerns, including those in this collection, tend to treat the subject out of the context of its social and cultural history. Replete with statistical or clinical data, the result is frequently a generic evaluation of the modern family with only some consideration of ethnic values. That which is peculiarly and normatively Jewish may be devalued, with greater stress upon the dislocation rather than the continuity of religious or cultural tradition.

However, data gathered from classic Jewish sources indicate that many of the selfsame stresses and conflicts facing the Jewish family today were well known centuries ago. Medieval Jewish communities were tightly structured by religious and social usage and generally barred from out-movement by inhospitable host cultures. It is scarcely surprising, therefore, that contemporaneous rabbinic writ deals extensively with intimate details of marital relations, childrearing responsibilities, divorce, and child welfare.

A portion of these teachings are codified in the context of filial obligation. By the early Middle Ages, systematic bodies of ethic and law emerged, alongside quasi-judicial findings and rabbinic dicta. These helped illuminate and elucidate formal attitudes

This paper is dedicated to the memory of my beloved mother, Mrs. Chana Schnall, z'l.

toward familial relationships. Such concerns as financial liability for parental care, intergenerational conflict, confrontations between other religious values and those of filial piety, and the care for the elderly and incapacitated parent, were filtered through the communal and social structures of disparate Jewries in Eastern Europe, North Africa, the Mediterranean region, Asia, and the Mid-East.

It is to these that we will turn in attempting to gauge and compare the values they reflect. The intent of this paper, therefore, is—

a. to offer an overview of filial obligation as it was understood in classic Jewish writings from biblical times to the early modern era;

b. to focus particularly upon the obligations of adult children toward their aged and infirm parents, with special regard to institutionalization and proxy care; and

c. to consider insights and inferences gleaned from the classic writings that may inform contemporary clinical and communal policy toward the needs of the elderly parent.

II.

The earliest normative references to filial responsibility in classic Jewish sources are scriptural. In both versions of the Ten Commandments, Israelites are adjured to "honor your father and your mother" (Exod. 20:12, Deut. 5:17). In addition, Scripture demands that we "fear every man his mother and his father" (Lev. 19:3).

Despite the clear injunctions to "honor" and "fear," Scripture is painfully terse regarding the definitions of these terms and the precise responsibilities of children toward their parents. Talmudic discussion, however, is far more elaborate. In several pages of legal debate, anecdote, and homily, the rabbis of the period (ca. 200–500 C.E.) review and evaluate familial values, gender roles, and filial obligation (Kiddushin 29–32).

They consider, for example, the reversal of mother and father in the scriptural references noted above. From this they infer that the natural tendencies of a child might be to honor his mother over his father, for she often "urges him with words." To emphasize the equality of their standing, father precedes mother in the verse requiring honor.

By the same token, when Scripture speaks of fear it reverses the order, placing mother first. Fathers may inspire fear in their children, not as disciplinarians, but rather because they "teach them Torah," suggesting awe and respect as a more accurate connotation. Therefore, the rabbis explain, Scripture now places mother first, i.e., once more to reinforce equity in the loyalty parents command from their children. Notwithstanding, there is a clear separation of function and role implicit in the talmudic schema: the mother who nurtures and the father who teaches.

Gender designations help define role and responsibility in other ways. The general sense of filial loyalty in the tradition suggests an equity in the status of mother and father. Yet classic authorities rule that in a direct and intractable conflict between them, the latter commands first loyalty. In the words of Maimonides: "Let him [the child] leave the honor of his mother and be busy with the honor of his father first, for both he and she owe honor to the father" (Hilchot Mamrim 6:14).

Two comments are in order. First, it is nowhere suggested that the needs of the mother are to be ignored. Rather the ruling reflects filial priority. Once the father's needs are fulfilled, the usual responsibilities toward the mother are reactivated. In addition, there is an important turnabout embedded in the tradition.

In regard to divorced parents, an extreme example of parental conflict, such constraints are removed. When parents are divorced, the tradition no longer assumes that "she owes honor to the father." Consequently, the demands of both parents upon their children are perfectly equal and priority is left to the discretion of the child (Hilchot Mamrim 6:14; *Yekar Tiferet* ad loc.).

Gender differences are also evident when children grow to their majority, marry, and raise families of their own. While the elements of honor and respect for parents continue, they are differentially applied. A son is expected to provide the same level of fear and honor as before his marriage. His new status as husband and father does not intervene upon these filial obligations (Schnall 1992).

For a daughter, however, it is taken for granted that her new role as wife and mother precedes and overrides her relationship with her parents. Save for the instance of her own divorce or widowhood, she must give first priority to her nuclear family. Consequently, the constraints of filial honor and respect are relaxed, even removed (Maimonides, Hilchot Mamrim 6:6; *Shulḥan Aruch*, Y.D. 240:7).

The point bears a contemporary irony. Notwithstanding the sentiments it expresses, it is a commonplace in contemporary society for married daughters to serve as primary caregivers to elderly, especially widowed parents (Turner and Karasik 1993; Cicerelli 1993; Suitor and Pilleman 1993). Indeed it has been noted that daughters-in-law frequently bear a disproportionate burden in caring for the parents of their husbands. It is more often the son who curtails his obligations of personal service (Merril 1993).

The Talmud also sets out to define and distinguish those actions or behaviors that denote fear (again, in the sense of awe or respect) and those reflecting honor. Consider the following:

> Our rabbis taught, what is fear and what is honor? Fear means that he [the child] must neither stand in his [the parent's] place nor sit in his place nor contradict his words. . . . Honor means that he must give him food and drink and cover him, lead him in and out.
>
> (Kiddushin 11b)

Apparently, the obligation of children was twofold. They fulfilled the requirement to fear through restrictions intended to reinforce the status of parents and the priority of their personal and social position. The focus was essentially negative or passive, i.e., what liberties may not be presumed. By contrast, honor implied an active service, filling personal needs and providing comfort and security.

The Talmud completes this portion of its discussion with a rabbinic debate regarding financial responsibilities. Given that children were required to provide food, drink, shelter, etc., were they also expected to cover any resultant expense? Conversely, did filial loyalty require an investment of personal service whose financing would be borne by the parent?

In fact, the matter appears to have engendered an early rabbinic controversy. In its treatment of the issue, the Jerusalem Talmud places the liability upon the children, ruling that in addition to providing personal service, they must also pay for the parent's maintenance (Kiddushin 1:7, Peah 1:1).

The more authorative Babylonian Talmud takes issue. It records the opinion rendered above, agreeing that children bear the expense of parental service to the extent that such care precludes their seeking income for themselves. They may not claim revenue or opportunity loss for the time invested in parental care. However, filial responsibility is fulfilled through personal service alone, and any expenses incurred as a direct result must be borne by the parent (Kiddushin 32a).

While this was accepted as normative by medieval codifiers of the tradition, they appear to have been concerned about the license that might be inferred from it. That the cost of parental maintenance is not to be borne by the children is reasonable, so long as the parents are financially able. But it would be unconscionable to permit children to ignore the needs of indigent parents.

This concern emerges at least as early as the eleventh century. Consider the words of Rabbi Yitzhak Alfasi:

> The rabbis ruled for Rabbi Jeremiah, some say for the son of Rabbi Jeremiah, in favor of those who hold at the expense of the father.

[Yet] when the son profits and the father has not, we compel the son and we collect from him in the form of charity and we give to the father.

(*Hilchot Rav Alfas* 13a–b)

Following the decision of the Babylonian Talmud, Rabbi Alfasi agrees that under model conditions filial responsibility is defined by personal service. However, though not required by the strict letter of talmudic dicta, when parents cannot care for their material needs, Jewish authorities will compel a child to fill the void.

As an aside, the term "charity" in this ruling ought not to be understood in the contemporary sense of voluntary philanthropy. Jewish tradition provides communal leadership with substantial powers of assessment and taxation to encourage support for local religious and social services. Though categorized as charity, Alfasi's finding is tantamount to a tax or penalty collected and transferred by a judicial body with the full sanction of religious law. His decision is accepted and codified by later authorities (e.g., Maimonides, Hilchot Mamrim 6:3; Ben-Yacov 50; *Shulhan Arukh*, Y.D. 240:3).

To summarize, the general parameters of filial loyalty demand that children exhibit respect through a variety of restrictions. They may not sit or stand in their parents' place, contradict parents, or enter into public debate with them. Children must also exhibit honor through personal service, e.g., feeding, clothing, and accompanying their parents. The consensus finds that parents must bear the expense of such service. If they are unable to provide for their own maintenance, children can be compelled by religious and communal authority to contribute to their care.

There are also gender differentials in the provision of honor to parents. In the classic two-parent family, precedence is given to the demands of a father. If the parents are divorced, however, discretion is left with the child. By the same token, the demands of filial loyalty fall harder—or at least longer—on the son. His responsibilities continue even after he has married and begun his own household. By contrast, a daughter's responsibilities are curtailed once she has married. Her primary loyalties are now directed to the more immediate demands of her own household.

III.

From these broad principles, interpreters of Jewish tradition made application to the structure and quality of family life confronted by their constituents. No concern was more poignant or of greater contemporary significance than the care of frail and elderly parents. Of course, filial obligations were uniformly understood to extend to old age, but questions arose regarding the limits of such obligations, if any. In an ethical system that places heavy emphasis upon personal service rather than financial support, could these responsibilities be transferred when parents were physically or emotionally incapacitated?

The classical sources lacked consensus. For example, consider a rabbinic homily written no later than the second century C.E. In Scripture, Abraham's commission to leave the place of his birth for "the land that I will show you" (Gen. 11:32–12:1) is preceded by the death of his father, Terah. Sensing a discrepancy in the text, Rabbi Yitzhak notes:

> Following the count to this point, he [Terah] is short sixty-five years. Rather, first, infer that the evil are considered deceased in their lifetime. And because Father Abraham feared that he would cause the Heavens to be demeaned, for others would say he was abandoning his father in his elder time. Said the Holy One: "You do I free from honoring father and mother, but I free no one else. And more, I will record his death before your departure."
>
> (Bereshit Rabbah 39:7)

The reference offers several relevant insights. It appears that nothing less than a dispensation from the Lord will free one of obligations to an elderly parent. Indeed, even then, the historicity of Scripture is compromised to maintain the integrity of the faithful against suspicions of their filial loyalty. Keeping with this theme, Maimonides rules that a convert to Judaism owes a measure of honor to his birth-parents, lest observers conclude that his new faith undermines the sanctity of family relations (Hilchot Mamrim 5:11).

In addition, that his father was evil does not appear to mitigate Abraham's responsibilities. Short of a Divine call, even sinners have a claim to honor and respect from their children. Later authorities ruled, however, that an evil parent loses many of his rights to filial loyalty, though uniformly they agreed that a child is adjured from striking or publicly insulting a parent, even if he be guilty of a capital crime (Hilchot Mamrim 5:12, 6:11; *Tur Shulhan Arukh*, Y.D. 240:18; *Shulhan Arukh*, Y.D. 240:18, 241:4: *Arukh ha-Shulhan*, Y.D. 240:18–39).

Thus we are left with the sense that filial responsibilities continue unrestricted throughout the life of the relationship, short of a commission from the Lord. Even the sinner has claims upon the loyalty of his children, claims that may override a desire to settle in the Holy Land.

And on its face, these responsibilities are not mitigated by mental incapacity. The Babylonian Talmud asserts that aberrant behavior on the part of parents is no license for a child to admonish or otherwise cause them shame. A parent who rends the clothes of a child or strikes him, or spits upon him as he sits in the council of nobles, must be borne in silence, if only as respect for the command of "He who spoke and the world was created by His will" (Kiddushin 31–32).

Nor may a child rebuke or show anger toward a parent who takes his purse of valuables and tosses it into the sea, though the consensus suggests that a child may seek recompense for a parent's actions in court or from the estate posthumously. But the thrust clearly indicates that even the irrational parent is deserving of honor and fear, and such is the sum of normative opinion among later rabbinic authorities (Hilchot Mamrim 6:7; *Tur*

Shulḥan Arukh, Y.D. 240:10, *Shulḥan Arukh*, Y.D. 240:8). However, Maimonides stakes new ground. He records:

> He whose father's or mother's mind is so damaged, must try to direct them according to their understanding, until the Lord have mercy upon them. And if it is not possible for him because they have been deranged in the extreme, he shall leave and command others to direct them as appropriate for them.
>
> (Hilchot Mamrim 6:11)

Characteristically, Maimonides provides no proof-text or precedent for his ruling. Commentaries to his work (*Kesef Mishneh* to 6:10) invoke a talmudic homily that is the mirror image of Abraham's dilemma detailed above. Thus:

> Rabbi Asi had an elderly mother. Said she to him, "I require jewelry" and so he provided her. Said she to him, "I require a husband" and he did her bidding. Said she, "I require a man as beautiful as you." And so he left for the Land of Israel.
>
> (Kiddushin 31b)

Reference to Rabbi Asi's experience offers vague support, at best. Rabbinic consensus takes his mother's demands to indicate incompetence. Yet, Rabbi Asi does not agonize over the decision to leave her. Absent a Divine call, he chooses nevertheless to move to the Holy Land rather than confront her irrationality. A child's obligations seem to be lifted when he is unable to contend with the incapacity of a parent.

In this vein, Rabbi Asi's actions are used as a counter in the confrontation of values between settling the Holy Land and fulfilling parental wishes. Contrary to Abraham's special dispensation, this reference suggests that a child may leave the home of a parent for the Land of Israel. The Talmud provides a conclusion to the homily that is relevant to this point.

Upon reaching his destination, Rabbi Asi learned that his mother had followed him. He asked of the rabbinic authorities if one might leave the Holy Land to greet a parent, suggesting that filial honor bore no automatic exemption from rule about dwelling in the Land of Israel. Faced with an inconclusive response, he lcft to meet his mother, who expired en route. Said Rabbi Asi: "Had I known, I would never have left."

With this as precedent, some contemporary authorities have ruled that (a) an adult child may leave an elderly parent to settle in the Holy Land, (b) a child who does so may leave the Holy Land for filial obligations only on a temporary basis with express intentions to return, and (c) once a parent has expired, filial piety may be an insufficient claim to leave the Holy Land even temporarily, e.g., to attend a funeral or visit a gravesite (Yosef 1981, pp. 249–254).

To the main point, however, Maimonides' license for a child to seek a proxy in caring for an incapacitated parent is not without detractors. Rabad of Posquières, for example, takes exception to the ruling. In his words: "I say that this is not a correct teaching. If [the child] will leave and abandon [the parent], whom will he appoint to care for [the parent]?" (*hassagot* on Hilchot Mamrim 6:10).

Though the statement is terse, there is much to be inferred. The ruling of Maimonides need not be understood in the framework of talmudic precedent. Its linkage to the anecdote about Rabbi Asi is tenuous at best and nowhere to be found in Maimonides' writings.

The suggestion that parents be left in the hands of a proxy is completely novel, and the assertion that this determination be based on the child's evaluation of the parent's demands flies in the face of talmudic and rabbinic writ. The preponderance of tradition suggests that the strain of caring for an impaired parent is no exemption from the filial service implicit in the requirement to honor one's parents, even if the expense of a proxy is borne by the child.

A later authority concurs, reevaluating the story of Rabbi Asi in defense of Rabad. He argues that a parent may be unreasonable without being incompetent, pointing out that nothing in the Rabbi Asi anecdote forces us to assume that his mother was deranged. Rather, he left her for the Holy Land because he could no longer fulfill her demands. Each hour with her, as he saw it, was a transgression of the requirement to honor.

> But if [parents] are deranged and require supervision in the extreme, sensibility does not provide that [the child] should leave and go. He is not required to fulfill their demands and he fears no punishment on their part, for they have no understanding. Therefore he is only required to feed and quench them and watch over them. How can he leave?
>
> (*Bayit Hadash*, Y.D. 240, s.v. *katav harambam*)

The argument introduces several new and complicating factors. In this formulation, parents who make unreasonable demands may provide their children with an exemption from their obligations. Using Rabbi Asi as precedent, the children may take leave and remove themselves from further transgression. Indeed, most authorities warn parents not to "make heavy the yoke upon their children or be overly demanding in regard to their own honor" (e.g., Maimonides, Hilchot Mamrim 6:8).

Further, as with any other member of the community, parents found to be incompetent lose moral and legal agency and the tradition no longer demands that their express will be followed. Only the essentials of fear and honor would inhere, and this is no license to leave them to the care of others. In fact, legal competence notwithstanding, a child may presume to refuse parental requests for specific food or drink if a doctor has deemed them dangerous (*Birkei Yosef*, Y.D. 240:15).

The point is buttressed with a bit of jurisprudential logic offered by yet another rabbinic thinker. If, as Maimonides asserts, a child may appoint others to care for his parents, then it appears that the parents' condition is manageable and amenable to treatment. Consequently, the child's responsibility is not mitigated. Who would be better aware of their needs and better able to care for them than the child himself? Conversely, if their condition is so extreme that it is impossible to care for them, then to what end will they be placed in the charge of others (Falk-Katz, Y.D. 240:2)?

To the mind of one medieval authority, a supporter of Maimonides, such legal abstractions miss the mark. The presence or absence of proof-text or talmudic precedent and the applicability of Rabbi Asi's anecdote aside, there are important clinical considerations that must be attended. For example, one part of a typical treatment program might require that a patient be physically manipulated, restrained, or subject to sharp verbal response.

No matter how appropriate, such therapy would be undignified, disrespectful, and therefore prohibited to a child. Under these circumstances, to insist that she/he continue to take direct personal responsibility for parents might actually impede their care and their progress. Rather than fulfilling filial obligations in cases of extreme impairment, children who refuse to place their parents in the care of others do them a profound disservice (Ben-Zimra 6:10).

Normative treatments of the subject infuse it with the power of religious law (*Shulhan Arukh*, Y.D. 240:10; *Arukh ha-Shulhan*, Y.D. 240:32). In specific cases of mental incapacity wherein familial systems are unable to provide adequately, Jewish tradition does countenance the appointment of a proxy—professional or institutional. This for clinical reasons and the demands of treatment or for jurisprudential reasons and the demands of legal precedent, and most likely for some combination of both.

However, one further qualification is in order. It is noteworthy that while normative Jewish tradition deals with forensic definitions of competence and moral agency, these rarely enter into our discussion. In light of the exemption from filial service in the words of Maimonides, "if it is not possible for him because they are deranged in the extreme," may a child seek a professional proxy to fulfill his obligations? Presumably, he still would be required to provide some care even through the duration of such a proxy.

Additionally, the impairment and incapacity of elderly parents and their institutionalization need not constitute a final determination. Regular review is in order to monitor their progress. Should professional opinion suggest that filial service is efficacious once more, it is reasonable to assume that the exemption would be lifted. The child would again be required to contribute to the equity and balance of the filial relationship.

IV.

Our analysis has dealt with the normative treatment of filial obligation, especially toward parents who are elderly and impaired. Historical data implicit in rabbinic rulings, communal enactments, biblical commentary, and social usage suggest that numerous other contemporary stress-points also differ by degree rather than kind.

Such findings have more than purely historical or academic import, however. They may serve to inform contemporary decisions in religious, cultural, and heuristic format. In particular, Jewish families that express loyalty to the tradition should appreciate that its ethics and values range far beyond the ritual. Decisions regarding the care of incapacitated parents or the financial needs of those who are indigent speak directly to the social and economic modalities by which modern families are organized. They also suggest that the relegation of Jewish culture and tradition to the realm of ritual observance is a very modern phenomenon that may not serve the best interests of the community or its faith.

Indeed, fitting traditional Jewish values and precedent to inform broad familial and communal decision may match the clinical rhythms and filial aspirations of those who are its objects in this study. Consider the pattern of but a handful of recent observations noted in eldercare.

In an essay included in this collection, Salamon calls our attention to the tendency for Jewish men, as they age, to attend religious services more frequently. Elsewhere, prayer has been found to play an important therapeutic role even among the "demented aged" (Abramowitz 1993).

Regardless of gender, the tendency appears salient beyond the purely ritual elements of Jewish affiliation (e.g., Kart 1987; Kart, Palmer, and Fleschner 1987). Research in Israel further suggests that religious structure appears to support the quality of relationship among elderly Oriental Jewish women, helping them to define their interpersonal domain, and to care for others (Sered 1989).

Classic Jewish attitudes toward filial responsibility may parallel other, more secular clinical judgments. Salamon's comments regarding reciprocity and social balance strike a particularly resonant note. He suggests that balance and reciprocity inform long-term relationships, contributing both to a sense of well-being and an ability to cope. For reasons of equity, obligation, or affection, such balance is vital.

The point can easily be rooted in Jewish tradition. Emphasis upon personal service suggests an equity with parental responsibility toward offspring. Even as parents in the classical family are required to feed, clothe, and care for their offspring, so too must an adult child provide service of the same nature. In both cases, relegating primary care to the hands of a proxy is considered neither the norm nor the normative.

By contrast, the first order of filial obligation is not financial. For reasons that are clinical as much as they are juridical, parents must provide for their own expenses, if possible. Elderly parents, especially those in need of the personal care of a child, may easily suffer a loss of pride, dignity, and self-respect. No longer able to contribute to the relationship, they may be shamed by this new-found dependency, notwithstanding the long investment they made against it. And so the tradition suggests that such credit aside, parents pay for their own needs and continue to maintain balance in their relationship with children, even as the latter express their filial piety through personal service.

Finally, data gleaned from normative Jewish writings may also speak directly to contemporary communal judgments. It is a commonplace, well documented by others in this volume, that the Jewish community in the United States is rapidly aging and that it has a higher proportion of elderly members than other ethnic groups in this country. Recent analysis of Medicare data suggests that this tendency increases with age, especially among Jewish males. A disproportionate number of Jewish females survive well into their senior years, by comparison with their Gentile sisters, but as age increases, the survival rate for Jewish males is still more disproportionate. Compared to the general population, increased proportions of Jews are reaching their eighty-fifth birthday and beyond, popularly called the "old-old" (Rosenwaike 1990, 1992).

The quality of life and the cost of care for this demographic cohort is of deep social, economic, and ethical consequence. While the American Jewish population at large is substantially above the national median for family income, economic hardship is more common among the Jewish elderly. For example, a recent study of the metropolitan New York Jewish community suggests that about 22 percent of Jews below the estimated poverty level were over sixty years of age. In addition, "some 44 percent of all poor Jewish households reported containing at least one elderly person" (Nova Institute 1993, p. 14).

Consequently, the Jewish communal agenda assumes a particular poignance when it confronts filial obligation and the costs of eldercare. The question of who pays for such care is crucial. For that agenda to reflect characteristically Jewish values, it behooves communal leaders and professionals to consider the precedents of their history and tradition, and include them as parameters for decision.

REFERENCES

Abramowitz, Leah. 1993. Prayer as therapy among the frail Jewish elderly. *Journal of Gerontological Social Work* 19, nos. 3–4:69–75.

Berman, Saul. 1984. Jewish tradition and filial piety. In *Honor Thy Father and Thy Mother: Perspectives on Filial Responsibility.* New York: Yeshiva University Gerontological Institute.

Bleich, J. David. 1981. Mental incompetence and its implications in Jewish law. *Journal of Halacha and Contemporary Society* 1, no. 2:123–143.

Blidstein, Gerald. 1975. *Honor Thy Father and Thy Mother: Filial Responsibility in Jewish Law and Ethics.* New York: Yeshiva University Press.

Chernick, Michael. 1987. Who pays? The talmudic approach to filial responsibility. *Journal of Judaism and Aging* 1, no. 2:109–117.

Cicirelli, Victor. 1993. Attachment and obligation as daughters' motivation for caregiving behavior and subsequent effect on subjective burden. *Psychology and Aging* 8, no. 2:144–155.

Kart, Cary. 1987. Age and religious commitment in the American Jewish community. In *Ethnic Dimensions of Aging.* New York: Springer.

———, Palmer, Neil, and Flaschner, Alan. 1987. Aging and religious commitment in a midwestern Jewish community. *Journal of Religion and Aging* 3, nos. 3–4:49–60.

Linzer, Norman. 1972. *The Jewish Family.* New York: Federation of Jewish Philanthropies.

———. 1986. The obligations of adult children to aged parents: A view from tradition. *Journal of Aging and Judaism* 1, no. 1:34–47.

Merril, Deborah. 1993. Daughters-in-law as caregivers to the elderly: Defining the in-law relationship. *Research on Aging* 15, no. 1.70 91.

Nova Institute. 1993. *Jewish Poverty in New York.* New York: Metropolitan New York Coordinating Council on Jewish Poverty.

Rosenwaike, Ira. 1990. Mortality patterns among elderly American Jews. *Journal of Aging and Judaism* 4, no. 4:289–303.

————. 1992. Estimates of the Jewish old-old population in the United States. *Research on Aging* 14, no. 1:92–109.

Schnall, David. 1987. *The Jewish Agenda: Essays in Contempoary Jewish Life*. New York: Praeger.

————. 1992. Antecedents of social casework in mediating domestic discord: Notes on the pursuit of *shalom bayit* in classical Jewish sources. *Journal of Jewish Communal Service* 69, no. 1:87–91.

Sered, Susan. 1990. Women, religion and modernization: Tradition and transformation among elderly Jews in Israel. *American Anthropology* 92: 306–318.

————. 1992. *Women as Ritual Experts: Religious Lives of Elderly Jewish Women in Jerusalem*. New York: Oxford University Press.

Singer, Shmuel. 1987. The challenge of honoring parents in contemporary social conditions. *Journal of Halacha and Contemporary Society* 14, no. 1:85–107.

Suitor, Jill, and Pilleman, Karen. 1993. Support and interpersonal stress in social networks of married daughters caring for parents with dementia. *Journal of Gerontology* 48, no. 1:1-8.

Turner, Katherine, and Karasik, Rosa. 1993. Adult daughters' anticipation of caregiving responsibilities. *Journal of Culture and Aging* 5, no. 2:99–114.

Yosef, Ovadia. 1981. *Shelot u-Teshuvot Yechaveh Da'at*. Jerusalem: Or HaMizrach Institute.

RABBINIC REFERENCES

Al-Fasi, Yitzchak (Spain and North Africa, 1013–1103). *Sefer Hilchot Rav Alfas* [HaRif] in *Talmud Bavli* (1974). New York: M.P. Press.

Ben-Asher, Yaakov (Germany and Spain, 1275–1340). *Tur Shulhan Aruch: Yoreh Desh* (1954). New York: Peninim Publishers.

Ben-Maimon, Moshe [Maimonides] (Egypt, 1135–1204). *Yad HaHazakah: Hilchot Mamrim* (1986). Brooklyn: Moriah Press.

Ben-Yechiel, Asher (Germany and Spain, 1250–1327). *Rabbenu Asher* in *Talmud Bavli* (1974). New York: M.P. Press.

Chumash Mikraot Gedolot (1971). New York: Friedman Publishers.

Epstein, Yehiel (Russia, 1829–1908). *Aruch HaShulhan: Yoreh Deah* (1987). Jerusalem: Wagshall Publishers.

Falk-Katz, Yehoshua (Poland, 1553–1614). *Drisha* in Ben-Asher, Tur Shulhan Aruch: Yoreh Deah (1954). New York: Peninim Publishers.

Ibn Daud, Avraham (France, 1125–1198). *Hasagot Haravad*, in Ben-Maimon, *Yad HaHazakah: Hilchot Mamrim* (1986). Brooklyn: Moriah Press.

Ibn Zimra, David (Egypt, 1479–1573) *Yekar Tiferet* in Ben-Maimon, *Yad HaHazakah: Hilchot Mamrim* (1986). Brooklyn: Moriah Press.

Karo, Yosef (Palestine, 1488-1575). Shulhan Aruch: Yoreh Deah (1965). Jerusalem: Hatam Sofer Institute.

———. Kesef Mishneh in Ben-Maimon, *Yad HaHazakah: Hilchot Mamrim* (1986). Brooklyn: Moriah Press.

Talmud Bavli (1974). New York: M.P. Press).

Talmud Yerushalmi (1981). New York: Otzar HaSefarim.

EPILOGUE

The pilot announced on the airplane's intercom that he had both good and bad news to report. "The good news," he said, "is that we are an hour ahead of schedule. The bad news is, *we are lost!*" From the psychosocial radar screen of American Jewish life, we seem to have similar news to report.

The American Jewish family today is living in an age that epitomizes the paradox of being "the best of times and the worst of times." Relatively free from the threat of antisemitic persecution, Jews have thrived and prospered in an atmosphere of freedom and tolerance that may be unrivaled in their long history. American Jews have arrived at a moment in time when they are not merely tolerated, but are accepted as integral to the variegated fabric of a pluralistic society.

Freedom and tolerance notwithstanding, the Jewish family has also been adversely affected by its profound engagement with the modern world. Having become so successfully integrated into mainstream American society, it is perilously close to losing its very distinctiveness as an institution capable of providing the unique Jewish environment that has traditionally fostered regeneration and survival. The contemporary Jewish family reflects instead all the manifestations of the troubled society in which it is embedded.

In this sense, modernity has not dealt kindly with the Jewish family. Its impact has not only affected the Jewish family's traditional norms, values, structures, roles, and functions, but its very identity as a *Jewish* institution.

In light of current concerns about the Jewish family's loss of distinctiveness and the ramifications of its enmeshment with modernity, the essays in this book explore some of the most salient psychosocial issues confronting the modern American Jewish family. The essays, embodying a diversity of perspectives and ranging in focus from broad overviews to detailed treatments of specific issues, are both descriptive and prescriptive.

Most of the essays reflect the point of view that the Jewish family has not fared well as a result of its widespread modernization and pervasive secularization. Several writers (Linzer, Levitz, Schnall, Danzig) underscore the fact that for centuries the traditional structure of the Jewish family was able to sustain an internal ethos rooted in religious values and complemented by social and community norms that effectively protected it from the world's prevailing ills. For the most part, however, with its transformation to the modern secular ethos, the Jewish family has lost its protective shield and is subject to the same deleterious forces as other families within the larger society.

Jewish family life in the past was certainly not problem-free. Jewish families have always suffered from a myriad of problems. Grinding poverty, unremitting unemployment, devastating illness, prejudice, discrimination, and murderous antisemitism have been integral to the Jewish life experience for thousands of years. From the perspective of battering forces and stresses, the Jewish past is clearly not a time to be romanticized.

The internal and external battering forces (Danzig) that are pummeling the integrity of the modern Jewish family are very different, however, and have given rise to a number of poignant observations reflected in several of this volume's essays.

No longer is the Jewish family immune to abuse, addictions, assimilation, and intermarriage. With its structure in flux, its values in question, its roles in transition, its functions unclear, and consequently its integrity weakened, the very survival of the modern Jewish family as an effective Jewish institution is being called into question.

Having lost the distinctive characteristics that allowed it to be both a buffer against external hostility as well as an arena for the nurturing of Jewish identity, the Jewish family is now in the throes of unprecedented turmoil. Problems previously thought to exist only in the gentile world have now become so pervasive in the Jewish community as to be considered commonplace. For millennia, Jews prided themselves on being immune to the toxicity of the world that surrounded them. They differentiated themselves from their gentile neighbors, not only in terms of religious beliefs, values, behaviors, education, language, and dress, but in terms of the very special quality of their domestic life. The secret of Jewish survival has indisputably always been rooted in these distinctive characteristics within the sacred precincts of the Jewish family. For the majority of contemporary American Jews, there is no longer anything distinctive about Jewish family life, and its vulgarization has consequently made it more vulnerable to all of society's ills.

In this volume authors Ruth Feldman and Rivka Ausubel Danzig provide an introductory examination of the changing norms, pervasive pressures, and stress points of contemporary Jewish family life.

Norman Linzer and Irving Levitz examine the impact of societal values on the internal ethos of the Jewish family. In an analysis of the ideological conflict between the societal values related to personal rights and the Jewish value of personal responsibility, Linzer argues that the impact of society's values on the contemporary Jewish family has profound implications for the increase of divorce and the decrease in fertility among modern Jews.

Levitz similarly examines the secular norms embraced by the majority of American Jews, with emphasis on those that directly affect their identity and survival as Jews. He explores the salient psychological antecedents that serve to propel the modern Western Jew toward assimilation and intermarriage. As a way of understanding how even individuals from Jewishly identified families nevertheless intermarry and assimilate, Levitz proposes a clearer conceptual basis for understanding the differences between Jewish identity and Jewish identification. Both Levitz and Linzer argue persuasively that the secularization of the American Jewish family has made it less stable and reduced its viability as an institution capable of perpetuating Jewish continuity and survival.

The ravaging effect of intermarriage on individual families is the focus of Mark Sirkin's essay. Sirkin's perspective emerges from his work with families and couples in crisis. His work reflects both the broad spectrum of personal issues that families and couples experience in the throes of intermarriage, and also the family-systems approach that he suggests as a way to help clients sort out the complexities facing them as a result of intermarriage.

In contrasting the essays by Levitz and Sirkin, it is instructive to note not only that the two writers describe different phases of the intermarriage process but that they prescribe stage-appropriate strategies for confronting that process. Whereas Levitz is concerned with primary prevention, namely, the development of a cognitive–behaviorally based Jewish identity that can prevent intermarriage from occurring, Sirkin focuses on a clinical strategy of secondary intervention, namely, family treatment when intermarriage is imminent.

ROLES AND RELATIONSHIPS

Several essays in this volume examine the effects of modernity on traditional roles and relationships within the Jewish family.

Guided by the values of self-transcendence, the primacy of responsibility over rights, and a strong, religiously based respect for parents, the traditional Jewish family has historically been characterized by an ethos of intense reciprocal filial support (Linzer, Danzig, Feldman, Salamon). With an increase in the average life span and the current low level of Jewish fertility, the demographics of the Jewish community are such that the elderly now comprise a larger proportion of the community (20 percent) than the proportion found in other ethnic groups (11 percent). What this means is that within the Jewish family there is a growing trend for fewer children to be responsible for the care of elderly parents for a longer period of time than in the past. With the increased burden of care subsequently placed on a middle-aged "sandwich" generation, the traditional Jewish ethos of support, filial responsibility, and parental respect is being challenged as perhaps never before.

Michael Salamon, in a broad-based examination of issues pertaining to the Jewish elderly, depicts a complex picture of aging within the context of the contemporary Jewish family. A ubiquitous theme reflected in Salamon's essay is that the more traditional the family structure, the more likely is filial support to be motivated by a sense of moral imperative and personal responsibility. Relatedly, Salamon cites several studies that conclude that the adjustment process itself is helped by more traditional rootedness. Jews who are more religious in their beliefs and behaviors tend to experience and report better overall adjustment to the aging process than their nonreligious cohorts. Religious faith appears to be a potent antidote to the losses and emotional stresses of aging, as tradition appears to provide a framework for effective care and support for aging family members.

In a related essay, David Schnall explores classic Jewish sources and provides us with a scholarly yet practical understanding of the principles of practice that have traditionally informed the care of elderly parents. He analyzes the complex relationship of children and parents from a traditional perspective and explores its ramifications for the contemporary Jewish family. In a changing world where family roles and functions are often unclear and undefined, and where the challenges of aging are more complex than in the past, traditional guidelines tend to serve Jewish families well.

Tradition and change is also the thematic framework for Francine Klagsbrun's essay on the changing roles of women and their effect on the quality of Jewish life.

The women's movement has affected Jewish family life in myriad ways. The majority of modern Jewish women are not only more educated than their forebears, but also more likely to be out in the workplace climbing the career ladder along with their male counterparts. Klagsbrun, in examining the experiences of the contemporary Jewish woman, applauds her achievements but thoughtfully examines the ramifications of these achievements. It may indeed be true that there are now more women scholars, professionals, and members of the workforce than ever before in Jewish history, but it is also true that Jewish women today are paying a heavy price for their hard-won achievements. With the emphasis on education and career, they tend to pursue career goals in lieu of early marriage. Consequently, when they are ready to bear and raise children they tend to be older and more prone to experience the frustrations and anguish of infertility than Jewish women in the past.

A number of essays make the observation that modernity has brought in its wake an increased incidence of domestic violence (Klagsbrun, Danzig, Feldman). Despite socioeconomic gains and greater independence, modern Jewish women remain more subject to poverty, experience greater stresses in marriage, and are more likely to suffer the pain of divorce and the burdens of single parenthood than their grandmothers.

Some of the issues raised in this volume are certainly not new in the annals of Jewish history. They were concerns even in the time of our forebears. The economic hardships and struggles of single parents in raising their families, the trauma of divorce, the pain of infertility, the high cost of Jewish education, poverty, prejudice, and discrimination—all of these would surely have been recognized by generations past as Jewish concerns. Our ancestors, however, would have been astounded by the degree and pervasiveness of these problems among contemporary American Jews.

Many current issues would simply have been beyond the ken of past generations. The shocking prevalence of child, spouse, and elder abuse, incest, drug and alcohol addiction, all within the precinct of the Jewish family, would have startled our most progressive-thinking grandparents into disbelief. They may have had problems, but of a very different sort.

The contributors to this book reflect in their work a concern and commitment to the Jewish family, not only as a system that provides nurturance, protection, support, and growth opportunities for its members, but as the ultimate guarantor of Jewish survival. In their diagnoses, descriptions, inquiries, analyses, and recommendations, the authors, in their own ways, contrast the state of the contemporary Jewish family with that of the traditional model. It was not the intent of any author to romanticize the traditional Jewish family or portray it as problem-free. The ideal Jewish family, if it ever existed, was, after all, a human entity, and as such was neither flawless nor without its share of dissatisfactions. It did, however, seem to provide considerably more in terms of Jewish values, family structure, stability, and sense of purpose than does its modern counterpart.

In the end, it is hoped that all of the descriptive contrasts, conceptual insights, and prescriptive recommendations found in this volume might serve as a way of providing guidance and perspective for those who are still concerned about the Jewish family and see it not only as the most central arena of Jewish life, but as the only hope for a Jewish future.

ABOUT THE
CONTRIBUTORS

Rivka Ausubel Danzig, D.S.W., is an assistant professor at the University of Pennsylvania School of Social Work, and formerly was a consultant at the Auerbach Central Agency for Jewish Education in Philadelphia. She received her M.S.W. and D.S.W. from the Wurzweiler School of Social Work, Yeshiva University where she was an assistant professor for five years. She spent a year at Bar-Ilan University and served as Lady Davis Professor at Hebrew University. Dr. Danzig has also worked in child- and foster-care agencies. She writes and lectures on the Jewish family, feminism, Jewish values, and Jewish education.

Ruth Pinkenson Feldman, Ed.D., teaches at Gratz College and serves as the early childhood consultant for the Auerbach Central Agency for Jewish Education in Philadelphia. Her doctorate from Temple University and M.S. from Bank Street concentrated in early childhood education. She has written numerous papers and monographs on early childhood education and other issues in Jewish family life.

Francine Klagsbrun, M.A. in art history, Institute of Fine Arts, New York University, author and lecturer, writes extensively on social, religious, and feminist issues. She writes columns for *Moment* and the *Jewish Week*, and is the author of a dozen books, including *Voices of Wisdom: Jewish Ideals and Ethics for Everyday Living* (Pantheon) and *Mixed Feelings: Love. Hate. Rivalry and Reconciliation among Brothers and Sisters* (Bantam).

Irving N. Levitz, Ph.D., Carl and Dorothy Associate Professor of Pastoral Counseling at the Wurzweiler School of Social Work, Yeshiva University, received his M.A. from the New School for Social Research and his doctorate in psychology from the Ferkauf Graduate School of Psychology, Yeshiva University. He directed the Clergy Program at Wurzweiler, and coordinated educational conferences in grief and bereavement and clergy burn-out. A psychologist in private practice, Dr. Levitz has published and lectured on a variety of Jewish and psychological subjects, including a seminal study of children of rabbis.

Norman Linzer, Ph.D., Professor, Samuel J. and Jean Sable Professor of Jewish Family Social Work at the Wurzweiler School of Social Work, Yeshiva University, received his M.S.W. from Wurzweiler, and his doctorate in sociology from the New School for Social Research.

He has been the acting dean and the chairman of the doctoral program of Wurzweiler. An editor of the *Jewish Social Work Forum*, Dr. Linzer lectures and writes extensively on the Jewish family, professional ethics, and social issues. All told, he has written over fifty articles and book reviews, and three books, the most recent, *The Jewish Family: Authority and Tradition in Modern Perspective*, (Human Sciences Press).

Michael J. Salamon, Ph.D., founder and director of the Adult Developmental Center in Woodmere, New York, is also a clinical supervisor at the New Hope Guild Community Mental Health Center. He received an M.A. and doctorate in psychology from Hofstra University, and has taught at Long Island University, Touro College and New York Institute of Technology. Dr. Salamon has published nearly a hundred papers, monographs, books, and book reviews on the elderly, health care, and family and marital counseling.

Mark Sirkin, Ph.D., is a consultant with the New York office of RHR International, a management-consulting firm of psychologists. He was formerly the director of the Robert Beren Center, Ferkauf Graduate School of Psychology, Yeshiva University and a clinical assistant professor in the department of psychiatry at the Albert Einstein College of Medicine. He received his M.A. and doctorate in psychology from the University of Connecticut. His numerous articles and presentations deal with intermarriage, cults, and families and other complex social systems.

David J. Schnall, Ph.D., Herbert H. Schiff Professor of Management and Administration at the Wurzweiler School of Social Work, Yeshiva University, received his M.S from Yeshiva University and his doctorate from Fordham University. Previously, he was professor of public administration at Long Island University and taught at City University, the State University of New York, and Fordham. Dr. Schnall is the author of over fifty articles and five books, the most recent being *The Jewish Agenda: Essays on Contemporary Jewish Life* (Praeger). He is an active consultant on human resource development and training for health, mental health, and social service organizations.